THIRD EDITION

Mentoring Matters

A Practical Guide to Learning-Focused Relationships

Laura Lipton   Bruce Wellman

Third Edition
MiraVia, LLC, Charlotte, VT

 *The Road To Learning*

 Follow us @MiraViaP

Page layout and cover design by Rebecca Manchester
www.RebeccaManchester.com

Mentoring Matters:
A Practical Guide to Learning-Focused Relationships

THIRD EDITION

by
Laura Lipton and Bruce Wellman

Every effort has been made to appropriately cite original sources. We apologize for any oversights in obtaining permission and would be happy to rectify them in future printings.

Microsoft, PowerPoint, and Windows are either registered trademarks or trademarks of Microsoft Corporation in the United States and/or other countries.

10 9 8 7 6 5 4 3 2 1

Printed in the United States of America

ISBN 978-0-9981770-1-4 Softcover

MiraVia, LLC
www.miravia.com

Dedication

To teach is to learn. We dedicate this book to the inquisitive spirit and boundless energy of beginning teachers and their committed mentors, who work together to make schools richer places for children and adults.

Acknowledgments

The term mentor originated with Homer, who, in The Odyssey tells of Odysseus, King of Ithaca. Upon leaving for battle in the Trojan War, Odysseus placed his son Telemachus in the care of Mentor, who served as a teacher and caregiver. In contemporary lexicon, the word "mentor" has become synonymous with a trusted advisor, friend, teacher, and wise person.

The mentors in our lives have been more than trusted advisors, friends, and teachers. They have been role models who have given us a vision of how we might behave and who we might become as we grappled with the professional challenges of beginning teaching, beginning consulting, and beginning our present partnership.

The influence of respected colleagues has been so profound that it is not possible to separate our work in this guide from their contributions to it. This is especially true of two masters who helped to shape the professionals we are today, and whose work is fundamental to our thinking. Our special thanks and deepest affection go to Dr. Arthur Costa, a beacon of integrity, authenticity, and self-directed learning; and to Dr. Robert Garmston, who embodies commitment, curiosity, and joy in work and life. These two guiding lights illuminate our personal and professional pathways and continue to blaze new learning trails. As our mentors, they constantly offer support, cognitively challenge, and facilitate our professional vision.

Our original work in mentoring, and the first edition of this book, would not have been possible without collaborations with our valued colleague, Carlette Humbard. Her high professional standards and deep commitment to improving education continues to inspire this new edition.

This third edition is the result of rich and multiple experiences and opportunities to share Mentoring Matters with skillful and committed educators across the globe. We have learned much from teaching this content to new and experienced mentors and by working directly with others who are doing similar work.

L.L. & B.W.

Contents

Contents *(continued)*

Contents *(continued)*

Tables and Figures

MENTORING MATTERS KEY CONCEPTS

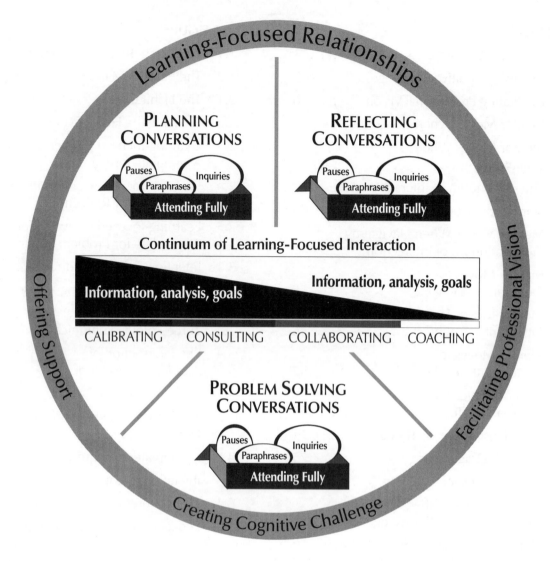

The diagram above, Mentoring Matters Key Concepts, illustrates the interrelated elements of learning-focused mentoring. Inside this book you'll find descriptions, examples, and practical approaches for applying these concepts.

Section 1: Three functions of a Learning-focused Relationship: Offering Support, Creating Cognitive Challenge, and Facilitating Professional Vision

Section 2: Structured Conversations for Maximizing Time and Attention: Planning Conversations, Reflecting Conversations, and Problem Solving Conversations

Section 3: Learning-Focused Conversations: A Continuum of Interaction

Section 4: Learning-Focused Verbal Tools: Pauses, Paraphrases, and Inquiries

In addition, this guide to learning-focused relationships includes information on teaching expertise and tools for accelerating the transition from novice to more expert practice for beginning teachers and their mentors.

Section 5: Facilitating Professional Vision: From Novice to Expert Teaching

Section 6: Strategies for Success

Section 7: Downloadable Resources

Section 8: References & Resources

PREFACE | Mentoring Matters: A Practical Guide to Learning-Focused Relationships

"As novice teachers enter the profession in increasing numbers, two clear needs arise. The first need is for quality induction programs that support newcomers so they will remain in the ranks of the teaching force long enough to develop classroom expertise. The second need is to develop the mentoring strategies, practices, and programs that provide the necessary supports and cognitive challenges to accelerate and ensure this professional vision."

— Kutsyruba, et al.

> "Sometimes, the experts forget they were once beginners. You must be gentle with beginners; they have great potential to be experts."
>
> - Lailah Gifty Akita

Debbie, a first-year teacher in an urban school, finds herself counting the days until the end of the school year. Five of her students have limited proficiency with English and four more experience mild disabilities. Surrounding her is an unending stack of forms, student assessment data, and the results from the first classroom observation by her principal. She reflects momentarily on her pre-service enthusiasm and her vision of being a teacher. Now she just wonders how to meet the differing needs of her students, complete the necessary paperwork, replenish the centers and activity stations scattered about her room, and prepare to strengthen her pre-and post-assessment techniques before next week's evaluation meeting.

Shonda is transitioning to teaching after a productive ten-year career as a medical technician. She has a passion for teaching biology. Her new principal is excited by the prospect of her being able to incorporate her real-world experiences into her teaching as a way of inspiring students to explore science related careers. While she is confident that she knows biology, she's less secure in her ability to make her favorite subject exciting and engaging for her students. While Shonda is drawn to the many rewards of teaching, she is also daunted by what she's heard about how taxing the work can be and how long hours are needed to do the job well. Sitting amidst a pile of resources materials, curriculum guides, and content area standards, she wonders if she has what it takes to make it in this new profession.

John has been teaching for ten years in a neighboring system but now finds himself in a new school with new colleagues. The beginning of the school year has always been highlighted by renewing connections with colleagues and establishing relationships with a new class of students. What was once a comfortable ritual is now filled with apprehension. John's knowledge and skills were well established in his previous environment, but now he feels the need to prove himself all over again. Adding to his concerns is the need to relearn logistical and procedural processes for matters such as ordering materials, acquiring equipment, completing attendance forms, requesting leave, and last but not least, getting paid. What are the everyday routines for this school? Who is in charge of specific activities? It seems as though he is two people—sometimes an expert and sometimes a novice.

Anna an experienced teacher, is beginning this school year with an additional responsibility. She is now a mentor for a beginning teacher in her school. Anna's first thoughts are of her own first year. She remembers feeling isolated, inadequate, and unsure as she faced that first set of students. How can she ensure that her beginning teacher's first experiences are different? She gets excited as possibilities and ideas begin to surface. That feeling soon turns to anxiety. Where should she start? Will she be able to solve all the problems that will emerge? Will she have answers to all the questions? Should she have all the answers? How can she support her beginning teacher and fulfill her own teaching duties? How will it all work?

The Evolving Landscape

Teaching has changed dramatically in the fifteen years since we published the previous edition of Mentoring Matters. Student and teacher demographics are some of the most significant drivers of these changes. The student population is and will continue to become more racially and ethnically diverse. An increasing percentage of students in poverty affects learning needs and influences both the social-emotional and political contexts that surround classrooms and schools. Rapid changes in technology and increasingly available digital devices contribute to the development of students' brains in ways that are just beginning to become apparent. The connected world shapes instructional design, classroom culture, and relationships with parents.

Further, many indicators suggest that the cohort of teachers joining the profession expect to have multiple careers. While many plan to remain in education, they don't plan to remain in the classroom. These new teachers will need to experience early success in meeting the learning needs of their pupils and to find the professional satisfaction that may entice them to remain in education. An effective mentoring relationship helps to produce these results.

The emergence of clear teaching and learning standards have greatly influenced our thinking in writing this edition. When mentors illuminate standards, they clarify the expectations for student achievement and teaching excellence. The ability to structure and facilitate learning-focused, standards-based conversations thus becomes the skill set to make mentoring matter.

Challenges of Beginning Teachers

From their first day on the job, beginning teachers are expected to perform essentially the same tasks as experienced veterans. The trial-by-fire method of casting novices into the fray of the classroom has been the traditional welcome into the teaching profession. However, there is an increasing body of literature and research regarding the importance of comprehensive teacher induction. Both this research and current practice indicate clearly that mentoring is an essential component in welcoming and retaining new teachers into the profession and supporting continual improvement in practice. New teachers often have a mistaken belief in the existence of some readily available package of skills and tools that can transform their classrooms into ideal learning environments. It is part of the mentor's role to debunk this myth and support novices in developing the capacity to make effective instructional choices, based on the intersection of learning standards and student needs.

Novices who participate in high quality induction programs that include a comprehensive mentoring component have consistently shown that they increase beginning teacher retention, improve student achievement, and reduce the waste of financial and human resources associated with teacher turnover. Beginning teachers that are effectively supported early in their careers have increased effectiveness in their classrooms, higher satisfaction, and greater commitment than those that do not experience these supports.

Comprehensive mentoring is part of a thoughtful induction program. Districts that consider the needs of beginning teachers and the educational and financial costs of not retaining good teachers realize that they are investing in the future and not just solving immediate personnel needs. Mentoring matters, but skilled mentors matter more. Not all good teachers make good mentors. Without targeted training in mentoring skills, they are usually ill-equipped to guide the development of novice teachers.

Beginning teachers flee the profession when they lack support. Thousands of teachers abandon their careers in the first five years. Among all beginning U.S. teachers in the 2007-2008 school year, 10% did not return to the classroom the following year. By the 2011-2012 school year, 17% of that cohort were no longer teaching (Ingersoll & Strong, 2011).

The Percentage of Novice Teachers in U.S. Schools

The data for the most recent school year available (2011-2012) indicate that on average 10% of the more than 3.1 million teachers in the U.S. have less than 2 years of experience. This varies greatly by state, with 23% of Florida's teachers being novices and only 5% of Washington State's and Rhode Island's teachers in this band. Nationally this works out to over 300,000 novice teachers serving close to 5 million students. Students in high-poverty or majority minority schools are most likely to have novice teachers.

The Condition of Education 2017

Without the formal role of mentor to define the veteran-novice relationship, new teachers are reluctant to ask for help, fearing the perception of incompetence. Caring, experienced colleagues are reluctant to offer help, for fear of appearing to interfere. Unwittingly, this double-bind often increases the isolation felt by first year teachers. Even with the role definitions, establishing and maintaining a learning-focused mentoring relationship is challenging. Yet the rewards of welcoming and guiding a colleague into our practice are fulfilling for the mentor, and the teaching profession-at-large.

This guide is designed to support the initiation, development, and maintenance of a fruitful, learning-focused experience for mentors and their beginning teachers. It is filled with practical tips, specific strategies, and menus of ideas that correlate to the developing needs of the novice teacher.

Exploring Our Assumptions About Mentoring

Learning-focused mentoring programs begin with both a shared vision and the identification of underlying assumptions and beliefs. These beliefs are the initial building blocks supporting and influencing the structure and expectations of the mentoring program. The goals of collaborative, growth-oriented, learning-focused relationships are based on the following five assumptions:

Induction is an investment in retention, integration, and continual growth.
The ways in which an organization initiates new members are an important aspect of its culture. Growth-oriented, learning-focused school cultures provide time and resources to welcome and nurture novices. While orientation and policy awareness are vital ingredients in an induction program, mentoring relationships are central to the success of developing and retaining effective practitioners. Mentoring is more than guiding the completion of induction tasks to satisfy certification requirements. Effective mentoring creates cohesive and collaborative instructional partnerships by establishing the norm of ongoing learning about and from teaching.

Emotional safety is necessary to produce cognitive complexity.
Attending to the emotional, physical, and intellectual environment of the mentoring relationship accelerates growth from novice to expert teaching. Mentors must construct a safe space, where verbal and nonverbal communication indicates full attention and high expectations, carefully balancing support with challenge. These components allow colleagues to share questions, concerns, information, and skill gaps in confidential, supportive, and productive interactions.

Mentoring relationships offer opportunity for reciprocal growth and learning.
Thoughtful conversations about educational practice establish forums for learning. Mentoring relationships provide opportunities for thinking out loud, sharing information, solving problems, and creating novel approaches to working with students. The learning is reciprocal, offering renewal for experienced teachers and increasing confidence for novices.

The central goal for mentoring programs is improved student learning.
Relationships that support beginning teachers must challenge them to examine instructional connections to student learning. Mentoring conversations provide a focus on internal and external data that are individually and collaboratively interpreted and translated into meaningful and thoughtful instructional activities.

A successful mentoring program will be integral to the implementation of other school and district initiatives.
Programs operating in isolation provide additional stress and management burdens to educators who are already struggling with time and resource issues. A mentoring program can, and should, work in concert with other initiatives. For example, information about instructional strategies may be framed within the context of content-specific learning initiatives already in place.

Four Benefits to Learning-Focused Mentoring

Mentoring offers multiple rewards, including the personal gains of renewal in working with a new practitioner, pride in contributing to a colleague's development, and increased consciousness for mentors about their own instructional practice. Learning-focused mentors serve to:

Improve instructional performance.
Expert teachers monitor their classrooms and flexibly adjust their actions in-the-moment and over time. Interactions guided by principles of effective teaching, within a learning-focused relationship, heighten new teachers' attention to student learning and alleviate beginning concerns.

Transfer the district policy, procedures, and educational philosophy.
Systems function most effectively when each member understands the goals, expectations, and operating values. Successful induction programs address the need for orienting the new teacher to the school system, school, curriculum, and community. Mentors also embody and transmit both their own and the school district's professional values.

Frame the professional learning journey.
Teaching is a lifelong learning adventure. No one knows it all or completely masters this craft. Advancements in neurobiology and cognitive psychology will continue to stretch the science of learning. New technology, curriculum updates, and an ever-changing student population all contribute to the ongoing need for continued professional renewal. Mentors are powerful models for novice teachers as they describe their own learning goals and help beginning teachers craft meaningful challenges of their own.

Promote norms of learning and collaboration.
The positive effects of peer learning emerge when schools embrace a culture of mentoring. These nurturing environments emphasize theory-driven instructional practice and the use of the collaborative processes to expand the knowledge and skill base. Given the emerging needs of the current student population, aligning whole schools for improving performance is fundamental to success for all.

Defining the Beginning Teacher

In designing the mentor's role to meet the needs of the new teachers within the district, it is useful to define some differences in personnel. The key distinction is between teachers new to the profession and more experienced teachers changing assignments. Novice teachers require different kinds and levels of support than transitioning veterans.

Literature in this area defines the induction period as the first three years of practice. Teachers who have classroom experience beyond three years, but have entered a new system, or a very different position in the same system, generally need information about, and orientation to, policy, facilities, procedures, and programs. Connecting with a mentor can also assist in the smooth integration with existing faculty. Educators making a grade or subject area change may simply need an orientation to the curriculum, materials, resources, and expectations of the new assignment.

While this guide has information and ideas to serve both groups, it is primarily designed to support mentors of novice, or beginning teachers. The reader will please note that while we are aware that both men and women compose the ranks of expert professionals in mentoring roles, we have chosen to use feminine pronouns as a convenience of form throughout this book.

Inside This Guide

Mentoring Matters: A Practical Guide to Learning-focused Relationships has been a valued resource for thousands of mentors around the globe. Feedback from these users and our own teaching, mentoring, and learning experiences are reflected in this new edition. As a result, you will find concrete examples of mentor/novice interactions, descriptions of specific mentor actions—or mentor moves—for each of the central concepts in this work, and end of section exercises called Awareness and Action for enhancing mentor skills. You'll also find QR code links to video clips illustrating essential ideas and skills. This third edition embeds a strong focus on teaching and learning standards as drivers of learning-focused conversations as well as current research on trends in education, developing expertise, and non-verbal and verbal communication skills. Key ideas and central themes for each section are described below.

Section One | The Mentor's Role

This section defines the mentor's role in a learning-focused relationship. It describes the importance of balancing support with creating cognitive challenge, along with ideas for facilitating professional vision. A calendar of options organized by the phases of the first year of teaching offers suggestions for anticipating the needs of beginners as the year unfolds.

Section Two | Structured Conversations: Maximizing Time and Attention

This section offers three structured templates for guiding planning, reflecting, and problem solving. It presents quick forms, time-saving strategies, and nonverbal tools for focusing attention and supporting learning. The section also offers tips for mentoring beginning teachers when it is difficult to meet in person.

Section Three | Learning-Focused Conversations: A Continuum Interaction

This section introduces four stances for learning-focused mentors, arrayed on a continuum from most to least directive. It suggests methods for balancing information with the opportunity to process that information. You'll find specific strategies for customizing learning-focused conversations that increase capacity and decrease dependency.

Section Four | Learning-Focused Verbal Tools

This section describes and illustrates verbal tools for creating emotional safety and producing complex thinking. It provides scaffolds for developing fluency with paraphrase and invitational inquiry, along with exercises for personal practice.

Section Five | Facilitating Professional Vision: From Novice to Expert Teaching

This section frames the journey from novice to expert teaching, articulating the major developmental differences between beginning and experienced teachers. It describes five spheres of expert teacher knowledge and seven lenses for assessing a beginning teacher's development offering tips for supporting professional growth throughout these developmental stages.

Section Six | Strategies for Success

This section offers practical tips and engaging strategies for supporting, cognitively challenging, and facilitating a novice's professional vision. These strategies are organized by time of year and required level of mentor commitment and effort.

Section Seven | Downloadable Resources

This section includes thumbnails of downloadable forms including: self-assessment rubrics for the mentoring relationship, personal mentoring skills, and beginning teacher needs; time-saving quick forms for focusing mentor/novice communication; and structured pages for beginning teacher reflection. You'll also find tools for establishing and monitoring a growth plan, enhancing learning from the text, and exercises to stretch your mentoring skills using video.

Section Eight | References & Resources

This section includes current research citations and online resources to support mentors in supporting their beginning teachers.

"New teachers quickly, but with no small amount of surprise, come to recognize that teaching is psychologically, intellectually, and physically arduous. New teachers also believe that they already ought to know how to do things which they have never done before. Another characteristic of new teachers is the sense that there are easily developed, immediately available strategies that can be used to transform their classes into some ideal condition. These beliefs and perceptions reflect an underdeveloped conceptualization of the inherent complexities of teaching."

— Murphy, Covin & Morey

SECTION 1 | The Mentor as Growth Agent

L EARNING-FOCUSED mentoring relationships make a significant emotional and intellectual difference in the induction experience for new teachers, as well as in their continuing professional practice. These clearly structured entries into the profession frame the learning journey from novice to expert teaching. Beginning teachers benefiting from skilled mentoring are more likely to:

- Effectively organize and manage instruction earlier in the school year
- Increase their efficacy as instructional problem solvers and decision makers
- Engage in collaborative professional exchanges regarding improving practice
- Remain in the teaching profession

First and Foremost

Who we are as mentors, how we mentor, and what we mentor about, are essential to meeting the current needs of beginning teachers. A central component in a learning-focused mentoring program is a clear understanding of the respective role and responsibilities of each participant. The most important function for mentors is to embrace a growth orientation, understanding that the work is to increase their colleague's effectiveness as professional problem solvers and decision makers. The most important function for beginning teachers is to embrace a learning orientation, understanding that the work is to examine their practice, both collaboratively and independently as a means to professional growth. This disposition for a collaborative relationship launches the multi-year journey towards expertise.

This process begins with establishing and maintaining a learning focus within the relationship. In this way, each party shapes and understands the nature and expectations of the mentoring interactions. We build on the work of Laurent Daloz (2012), suggesting that a mentor's role within such a relationship is to balance three functions:

- Offering support
- Creating cognitive challenge
- Facilitating a professional vision

These functions can operate independently in specific situations, but in the greater context of the relationship they must be interconnected. <u>Balancing these three elements energizes growth and learning</u>. Support alone will provide comfort but may encourage complacency. Cognitive challenge without support may increase anxiety and fear of failure. Support and cognitive challenge without vision may leave new teachers wandering on a journey looking only at the ground beneath them, but not the road ahead.

Plate spinning was a classic vaudeville routine, and these days, a street act. Envision a performer balancing multiple plates and moving back and forth to keep them simultaneously spinning (See Figure 1.1: Balancing the Three Functions). Once the plates are rotating, the performer does not return to each plate in sequence, but steps back to determine which plates might be losing energy and spins those. That is, there is balance throughout – some plates maintain their momentum while others need a boost. So it is with mentors as they provide the three functions described below. There is no correct starting point or sequence to these functions. Attending to the balance of all three is important. Skillful mentors pay attention to the needs of their beginning teacher and offer input accordingly.

Figure 1.1 Balancing the Three Functions

Offering Support

Support for the new teacher occurs in four distinct categories: emotional, physical, instructional, and institutional. Sometimes the novice needs a shoulder to cry on, a hug rewarding an especially exhilarating success, and every range of emotional support in between. Often, the support is physical—perhaps tackling the room arrangement, moving desks and setting up learning centers, creating classroom displays, establishing web connections, or even carting books for a thematic unit from the media center. Instructional support includes contextual application of teaching and learning standards, content area resources, and practical suggestions based on current research and years of rich experience. Institutional support includes guidelines for applying organizational policies and procedures and tips for navigating day-to-day routines, events, and expectations.

Instructional Support includes:

- Establishing classroom routines
- Managing student behavior
- Differentiating instruction
- Developing formative assessment strategies
- Planning and pacing lessons
- Interpreting curriculum

SUPPORT

- · Emotional
- · Physical
- · Instructional
- · Institutional

Institutional Support includes:

- Preparing for observations and evaluations
- Maintaining student records
- Acquiring resources
- Managing non-classroom duties
- Implementing school-based initiatives
- Following leave or attendance policies

Table 1.1 Offering Support

Mentor Move	What is it?	Might look/sound like
Attend fully	Respectfully listening when our partner needs to share concerns, frustrations, experiences, and new ideas.	Sitting side by side–no barriers. Put cell phones away. More beginning teacher talk than mentor talk. Mentors mentally bracket their own internal distractions.
Respond empathetically	Acknowledging feelings, and when appropriate, sharing relevant concerns, frustrations, and experiences.	*"That can be really frustrating."* *"That's a common concern at this time of the year."* *"I struggled with a similar issue early in my teaching."*
Create a safe space	Attending to the verbal and nonverbal communications that establish rapport and support thinking.	Pausing frequently to allow for thinking time. Asking more than telling. *"Let's look at this student's work to see where she's met the writing standards."*
Coordinate schedules	Agreeing on and protecting pockets of time that work for both parties. Establishing agreements for addressing pressing personal or professional concerns.	*"I think we should meet every other week – would that work for you?"* *"Let's protect some regular times/places that will work for each of us."* *"Let's establish some guidelines for dealing with pressing issues or concerns."*
Offer resources	Providing time, energy, materials, and strategies to ease the challenges beginners face.	*"Let's meet in your classroom after school to set that up."* *"As you prepare for that unit, I'll put together a few resources that might work well for your students."* *"I'll forward some web links on that topic for you to review."*
Provide information	Clarifying the practices and policies of the school and district to facilitate induction into the professional community. Sharing expertise and resources about the craft of teaching to support the development of sound educational practice.	*"Given this issue, there are a few things you need to consider. . ."* *"I've highlighted a few sections of the induction manual that you should pay particular attention to."* *"Let's create a calendar of critical deadlines in the first semester and set up some prep time in advance of them."*

Creating Cognitive Challenge

In our experience, mentors devote most of their time to spinning the support plate. However, unless support is balanced with cognitive challenge, we rob new teachers of the opportunity to grow and learn.

If our goal is to nurture independent, effective practitioners, then it is critical to develop the thinking patterns of increasing expertise: envisioning, monitoring, reflecting, and applying their learning to their classroom practices.

Growth requires that beginners develop the capacity to employ and adapt expert information within the context of their own classrooms. This development includes independently making meaning of new information and experiences. This learning enables new teachers to utilize, refine, and adapt strategies to meet student learning needs. Skillful mentors scaffold this growth process through their learning focused interactions.

Learning-focused relationships balance the support function with cognitive challenge to promote continual attention to improvements in practice. The table below illustrates five examples of creating challenge in a learning-focused relationship (See Table 1.2: Creating Cognitive Challenge).

CREATING COGNITIVE CHALLENGE
- Goal-driven
- Data-focused
- Thought-provoking

Facilitating Professional Vision

For beginning teachers, it is often difficult to project past the most immediate experience. There are no reference points for envisioning student growth or positive developments in the classroom environment. As a result, mentors need to help set reasonable expectations and reinforce the idea that present choices create future possibilities. The day-to-day operation of a classroom is generally new territory for the novice, so it is often necessary to illuminate the learning pathways (See Table 1.3: Facilitating Professional Vision).

*"We don't learn to teach;
We learn from our teaching."*

Facilitating the development of a professional vision early on fosters the belief that a teaching career is a learning career; teachers are lifelong learners who engage in continuous improvement. Promoting this function establishes a picture of sound educational practice and high expectations. It reminds us that we don't learn to teach; rather we learn from our teaching. Facilitating vision begins on day one of the mentoring relationship, balanced with the functions of Offering Support and Creating Cognitive Challenge.

One way to think about yourself as a growth agent is to imagine the colleague you would like to have teaching next door to you. With this person in mind, create a list of the knowledge, skills, and dispositions of your ideal neighbor. Then, note the various approaches you might take to help your colleague develop these resources. You will most likely find yourself crafting lists of ways to provide support, ways to intellectually challenge, and ways to model and foster an emerging vision as a professional.

FACILITATING VISION
- High expectations for self and students
- Lifelong learning
- Professional identity

Mentoring moments can be isolated action or part of an intentional approach to building expertise. Mentors need to be responsive to the immediate needs and energy of their new colleague as well as attend to their response patterns over time. Monitoring which plates you are spinning, when, why, and how often will help you identify your own habits and increase your consciousness about the choices you're making as a growth-oriented mentor.

Table 1.2 Creating Cognitive Challenge

Mentor Move	What is it?	Might look/sound like
Engage in goal-driven learning	Based on the new teacher's concerns, needs, and interests, identifying learning goals, and using the Planning Template to structure goal-driven conversations.	*"As you anticipate this first semester, what are some specific goals you want to focus on?"* *"Given your progress with classroom management so far, some new goals you might consider are. . . "*
Maintain a focus on student learning	Assisting in analyzing formative and summative student performance information, discerning patterns, and determining cause-effect relationships.	Explore samples of student work to focus conversations. *"The examples that you're using in this unit may be causing confusion for kids who have a different cultural background than yours."* *"Let's compare this month's reading data to last month's to assess your students' progress."*
Structure rigorous examination and analysis of practice	Applying the Planning and Reflecting Templates to focus and guide conversations (See conversation templates, pp. 30-32). Considering the beginning teacher's decisions and experiences and exploring causal factors for both positive and negative results of instructional choices. Assisting in identifying and articulating criteria for choices and outcomes.	Share the conversation templates with your beginning teacher prior to scheduled conversations. *"Given the responses on these exit slips, what's your hunch about what may be causing gaps in understanding for some of your kids?"* *"Let's brainstorm a list of options with pros and cons for each."*
Engage in problem solving as a teaching/ learning tool	Forging problem solving partnerships, brainstorming options and generating solutions. Structuring conversations by applying the Problem Solving Template (See p. 32).	Frame concerns as problems to be solved. Teach and model the Problem Solving Template to your beginning teacher to encourage independent application. Think aloud: *"When I see this kind of thing happen, some questions I consider are. . . "*
Develop norms of experimentation and reflective practice	Building connections between current theory and classroom practice. Constructing and conducting action research projects based on the new teacher's concerns, learning goals, and interests.	*"How do your own observations of student behavior fit with what this article is suggesting?"* *"Let's each try this new comprehension strategy and compare results."*

Table 1.3 Facilitating Professional Vision

Mentor Move	What is it?	Might look/sound like
Frame the journey from novice to more expert levels of teaching	Referencing teaching and learning standards and related rubrics to set high, yet achievable, expectations for the beginning teacher.	*"As we look at the standards for responding to students, let's clarify some differences between level two and level three."* *"As you imagine your own teaching six weeks from now, in what areas would you like to have greater confidence and skill?"*
Envision an equitable, identity-safe classroom focused on high levels of learning for all students	Modeling and articulating dimensions of a powerful classroom climate: strong relationships between teachers, students, and their parents; responding to students respectfully; and communicating belief in their capacity to learn. Painting the bigger picture of content integration: teach subject areas with culturally relevant, real world applications; using technology to connect to the wider world.	*"What are some things you monitor to know that students feel safe in your classroom?"* *"It's important to connect with parents early in the school year. Here are some strategies and tips for you to choose from for getting started with that."* *"Let's generate some specific examples that your students should be able to relate to for the next two social studies units."*
Create collaborative opportunities with other beginning teachers, their mentors, and within the faculty	Encouraging your beginning teacher's participation during grade or department level planning meetings and PLC's. Creating a community by orchestrating learning meetings with other mentors and their beginning teachers.	Host early morning gatherings for coffee and conversation about teaching. *"Let's sit together at the next PD session to process and apply new learning."* Coach your beginning teacher about ways to get their voice heard at meetings.
Model your own professional learning journey	Sharing your vision for your own classroom; articulating your own learning goals and the thinking behind them. Sharing professional reading or blogs and websites you find useful.	Do a think aloud classroom tour of your own classroom: share some of the things you've learned, your reasoning for your choices, and what you're hoping for. *"Given our conversation today, I'll email some links to related resources you might find useful."*

"Mentors need to help set reasonable expectations and reinforce the idea that present choices create future possibilities."

Recognizing and Meeting the Needs of Beginning Teachers

Beginning teachers' needs vary widely, as each novice brings a different perspective, experience, and knowledge base about teaching. Further, there are differences in cultural competency, preferred methods of problem solving, learning styles, and educational philosophies. However, there are some generalizations that can be made about the needs, expectations, and emotional phases during the first year of teaching.

The struggles of a new teacher in the twenty-first century are not that different from those in the early to mid-1900s. Several threads appear in the older literature on beginning teacher concerns: classroom management, student discipline and relationships, motivation, assessing and adapting to the needs of individual students, and functioning in an unsupportive environment (Wey, 1951; Johnson & Umstattd, 1932).

More recent studies on beginning teacher concerns align with this literature (Goodwin, 2012; Covert, et al., 1991). These studies identify concerns about students: controlling and managing, motivating, evaluating, and differentiating instruction. They also point to concerns about managing time: for planning, scheduling, completing work load, and balancing personal and professional life. Other concerns include relationships with colleagues, administrators, and parents. As we might imagine, beginning teachers worry about knowing what to do, when to do it, and whether or not they will do it well.

Phases of First Year Teaching

Ellen Moir, Director of the New Teacher Center at the University of California, Santa Cruz and her colleagues, have identified a series of mental and emotional challenges that occur in developmental phases across the first year of practice. They note that while every new teacher does not go through this exact sequence, these generalizations are a useful map for predicting and responding to the needs of novices. Under stressful circumstances, it is not uncommon for new teachers to briefly revert to previous phases. The six phases described in their work are: Anticipation, Survival, Disillusionment, Rejuvenation, Reflection, and Anticipation (Moir, 1999).

For novices, it is useful to understand that these phases are likely to occur as a normal part of their first year in teaching. As mentors, awareness of and sensitivity to these phases helps us to maintain a developmentally appropriate balance of support with cognitive challenge while facilitating professional vision.

Figure 1.2 The Phases of First Year Teaching

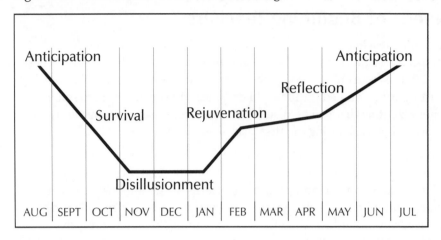

Anticipation

It is August and Janice is excited and anxious about the beginning of her first school year as a teacher. She is confident of her knowledge and has a passion for making a difference in students' lives. She can't wait to set up her room and organize materials. It will definitely be exciting to have a classroom of her own.

New teachers begin to anticipate their first year of formal work during their student teaching experiences. They enter their classrooms with a commitment to making a difference and an often vague and idealistic sense of how to reach their goals. Major concerns at this time are setting up the classroom, locating teaching materials, establishing relationships with colleagues, support staff, and administrators, and establishing relationships with students and parents. The press of tasks and the emotional rush of new responsibilities often propel novices through their first weeks on the job.

OFFER SUPPORT
Offer support during the Anticipation phase by providing information regarding materials, procedures, first day activities, and mandated paperwork for opening school. Set aside time to think out loud about your own strategies and rationales for room arrangements, first day activities, contact with parents, and support services. Collaborative opportunities may present themselves as you jointly plan for the first day or week of school.

CREATE COGNITIVE CHALLENGE
Maintain a learning focus by having a goal-setting conversation. Establish some initial goals for learning and for the mentoring relationship. Use national, state, or district standards combined with the novice's assessment of needs (See Section 7: Beginning Teacher Self-Assessment Inventory) to be sure the goals are relevant and reasonable. Discuss ways that you will monitor your progress and celebrate your successes.

FACILITATE PROFESSIONAL VISION
Ask your beginning teacher to articulate his or her idea of the ideal teacher. Share your own vision of professionalism. Expand the conversation to define productive learning environments and connect to the established goals. Remember to balance long-term thinking with support in the short-term. Assure your colleague that for now, it's fine to take it one day at a time.

Survival

It is Saturday night, September 30, and the realities of being a teacher are beginning to sink in. Janice is spending at least half of each weekend and most weeknights trying to keep up. She struggles with managing lesson plans, providing written feedback for students, record-keeping, parent meetings, and progress reports. She wonders if she really can do it.

The realities of the day-to-day work of the classroom soon bear down upon new teachers. They are faced with many different problems for the first time and have few of the routines and tricks-of-the-trade in their repertoires that help veteran teachers conserve time and energy. Most are running hard to stay in place and have little time for reflection or advanced planning. Many new teachers spend up to seventy hours a week on schoolwork. Often the core curriculum materials are unfamiliar and the novice teacher is only one or two lessons ahead of the class in preparation for future lessons. There is a constant need to learn the curriculum, develop instructional plans, learn and develop assessment systems, correct student work, and develop and gather materials. Many novices do not accurately anticipate the amount of work their chosen profession requires, but most manage to maintain their energy and commitment to student learning during this phase.

OFFER SUPPORT

Offer support during the survival phase by sharing materials and management tips. Time is precious and may not best be spent reinventing the wheel. Share tips for establishing routines and managing the activities of the day. Keep it learning-focused by thinking aloud about your choice points and purposes. You may wish to keep note cards handy during the day to record effective techniques that may be unconscious and automatized for you, but would be useful to share with your beginning teacher. Attend fully and listen empathetically as frustrations and concerns arise. As appropriate, invite your new colleague to observe in your classroom, or offer to model and debrief a lesson.

CREATE COGNITIVE CHALLENGE

Ask questions that help your beginning teacher recognize effective choices. Offer your ideas as a menu of options and generate criteria for choices. Ask your colleague to share thoughts about what might work best, and why. Gently challenge by asking your beginning teacher to keep a structured Reflection Journal (See Section 7: Downloadable Resources) and use the recording to focus your future conversations.

FACILITATE PROFESSIONAL VISION

Celebrate the goals already achieved (or sub-sets of them) and set new ones. Have conversations about what drew you to teaching, what's been important and/or rewarding to you so far. Focus your conversations on short-term accomplishments, the next week or the next unit. Create descriptions of what students should be doing between the present and the upcoming holiday break.

Disillusionment

Everything seems to be going wrong. The lesson that Janice's principal observed did not go as she had planned. The experiments did not work, the students did not participate, and she lost the supplemental handout for the integrating activity. Maybe she should never have taken this job, or even become a teacher. Maybe it is not too late to find another career.

After working seemingly nonstop for six to eight weeks, new teachers often hit-the-wall, entering a phase of disillusionment. This phase varies in intensity and duration as novice teachers begin to question their commitment, capability, and self-worth. These factors, combined with fatigue, can weaken immune systems. It is not uncommon for new teachers to get sick at this time.

Several temporal events add to the tension and stress experienced by new teachers at this point. The first round of parent conferences trigger stage fright and concerns about parents questioning both their competence and character. Holiday events soon follow with both time demands that cut into preparation for class and anxiety about relationships with parents. And the first formal evaluation by the principal occurs. Lack of familiarity with the process and, in some cases, the principal, adds to the stress load. Most often, the new teacher over-prepares a showcase lesson that consumes most of whatever planning time was available.

It is not uncommon for classroom management concerns and the needs of specific students to occupy much of the novice's attention during this phase. Routines and response patterns are not yet firmly established and mentors often find their counsel is sought and or required in these matters. Deeper issues of teaching and learning often have to wait until these issues are resolved or stabilized.

This phase is often the toughest challenge the first year teacher has to overcome. Self-doubt and pressures from family members and friends complaining about the time that teaching seems to take away from their relationships add weight to the burden new teachers carry.

OFFER SUPPORT

Continue to assist by sharing materials and tips for managing paperwork and conserving energy. Focus on what has been accomplished and learned to this point. Assist in the abandonment of unnecessary or ineffective routines and procedures. Collaborate by jointly planning for upcoming events. Think aloud regarding parent conferences and first semester assessments and grading.

Acknowledge feelings of inadequacy without dismissing them by suggesting that they will just go away. Check in often and watch for cues from your beginning teacher regarding needs. Remind and assure your colleague that this phase is a predictable part of learning to teach and is finite.

CREATE COGNITIVE CHALLENGE

Create cognitive challenge by helping your beginning teacher learn from experience. Use formative student performance data to identify positive results, explore beginning teacher choices that are producing these results, and strategize ways to amplify them. Continue to use structured Reflection Journals and quick forms to focus conversations (See Section 7: Downloadable Resources). Pay close attention to signals that you're pushing your beginning teacher beyond whelm into overwhelm.

FACILITATE PROFESSIONAL VISION

Facilitate professional vision by asking your beginning teacher to identify some examples of growth thus far and share specific, concrete things you have observed. Debunk the myth of professional certainty. Remind your beginning teacher that learning to teach is a continual process of purposeful experimentation, reflection, and modification. Emphasize that there are productive options, based on the best knowledge at the time, given the context of the situation.

Continue to connect the beginning teacher with other staff members, building a sense of community.

Rejuvenation

Wow! The job seems much more doable after two weeks away. Time away has allowed Janice to reconnect with friends, family, and herself. As she reflected on the first half of her year, she was amazed at how much she had accomplished and learned. Beginning the second semester, routines are in place and her expectations are much more realistic. As she looks at the calendar, she's delighted to have made it through the first half of the year and feels more optimistic about pacing and planning in this next semester.

For teachers on a traditional calendar, the winter break marks a transition in the pace and flow of the school year. Time away with family and friends reminds new teachers of their life outside of the classroom. Rest and relaxation re-energizes body and soul. With new outlooks come a glimmer of perspective and an emerging sense that this is a learnable profession, one that with time and attention, can be mastered.

Many novice teachers return from break with a clearer understanding of the realities of their classroom, the system in which they work, and ways to access available resources. They begin to have a small sense of their accomplishments as well.

Confidence in routines and relationships increases as the novice automatizes patterns for behavior, time, and instructional management. These, in turn, free time and energy for explorations of curriculum development, new teaching strategies, and longer term planning.

This phase tends to last into the spring with a few bumps and surprises along the way. One example is the pressure of preparing students for high stakes testing. These demands can cause a temporary reversion to the emotions and behaviors of the survival phase. As the end of the year appears on the horizon, concerns emerge about getting everything covered and everything done. Worries often arise about students' academic performance and novices may question their own instructional competence.

OFFER SUPPORT
Continue to celebrate, share, and mark goals achieved and milestones passed. If there is an emotional dip, restore resourcefulness by increasing direct consultation—offer explicit tips and strategies for addressing any identified pressures. Coordinate schedules to be sure that time with you is seen as offering resource not creating additional pressure.

CREATE COGNITIVE CHALLENGE
Focus cognitive challenge on instructional outcomes and cause-effect results. Inquire about new learnings and applications. Collaborate in analyzing student data. Continue to demonstrate and debrief instructional practices relevant to the emerging learning of your beginning teacher. Plan for

professional development opportunities and mutually construct implementation and evaluation plans for trying out new ideas. Meet and discuss the results and learnings from implementation. Engage in conversation cycles of planning, observation/data collection, and reflection.

FACILITATE PROFESSIONAL VISION
Collaborate with your beginning teacher— talk about the learning thus far and consider what's working well and what adjustments might be helpful. Try something new and ask your beginning teacher for feedback.

Reflection

Three weeks and counting! Janice recognizes the tremendous amount of growth she's experienced this year and feels pride in her accomplishments. As she thinks back, there are things she would never try again or would choose to do very differently. Next year will be exciting. She will not be the newest kid on the block and she has a workable plan for managing time and tasks. Janice also has greater comfort with content knowledge and setting expectations for students.

The last weeks of the first year are a time for reflecting and taking stock. Mentors reflect with novice teachers, helping them to remember all they have learned, what worked, what was modified, what was set-aside, and to consider growth goals for the following year.

End-of-year routines require time and energy at this phase. Parent communication, closing up the classroom, and a mountain of paperwork demand attention to detail. For many, the emotional leave-taking from the first class or classes marks this moment in time.

OFFER SUPPORT
Offer support during the reflective phase by providing information and tips regarding end-of-year events and paperwork. Share your routines for organizing end-of-year tasks. Make a gift pack of colored markers, tape, and stickers for labeling boxes. Start a list of items to order for next year.

CREATE COGNITIVE CHALLENGE
Use data to do a gap analysis. Make connections between what was expected, what was desired, and what actually occurred. Use the Reflecting Template (See Section 2: Structured Conversations: Maximizing Time and Attention) to structure a learning-focused conversation reviewing the second semester: surface insights, applications, and goals for the coming year.

FACILITATE PROFESSIONAL VISION
Explore student successes and mark the specific turning points for them and your beginning teacher. Share high points and low points and notice patterns or categories. Collaborate on constructing a professional growth plan for the coming year.

And Celebrate!

The Calendar of Options on the next few pages offers an array of ideas for a learning-focused first year organized by phases of beginning teaching, and research on the concerns of new teachers.

This calendar offers a menu of activities, correlated with time of school year, the developmental phases of beginning teachers (Moir, 1999), and Frances Fuller's pioneering work on stages of concern. In her research with beginning teachers, Fuller (1969) defined the phases of concern as Self, Task, and Impact. Self concerns involve feelings of adequacy, questions of ability, and potential effects on personal time and lifestyle; surfacing questions such as "Can I do this?", "What might happen if I can't?", "What does this mean for me?" Task involves management concerns such as scheduling, sources of materials, and many logistical issues, surfacing questions such as "How long will this take?", "Where do I find. . .?", "Am I allowed to do this?" Impact addresses concerns for others, including students, colleagues, and the school community. Questions that occur in this stage include "How will this choice affect my students?", "What are some ways I could support my team?", "How can I improve on this plan?"

It should be noted that these activities are provided as a menu of possibilities, and not a mandatory list. Activities marked with an *asterisk are described in detail in Section 6: Strategies for Success.

Calendar of Options

AUGUST
At least two weeks prior to school beginning

PHASE	CONCERN
Anticipation	Self

- Phone, email, or send personal note to make informal contact
- Informal get-acquainted meeting
- Joint Planning Session*
- Informal sharing of teaching materials, weblinks, files, classroom displays, etc.
- Share Incredible Ideas Scrapbook*

AUGUST
Week prior to school

PHASE	CONCERN
Anticipation	Self

- Share school plant layout, discipline policies, location, and availability of resources/materials, etc.
- Clarify record-keeping/management procedures
- Check for readiness of texts, kits, equipment, etc.
- Begin a Collaborative Staff Development activity*
- Share a Welcome To. . . Basket*
- Schedule a Meet, Greet, and Share*

SEPTEMBER
First Day of School

PHASE	CONCERN
Anticipation	Self

- Informal check-in and mutual sharing
- Have, or schedule, a New Teacher Luncheon/Shower*

Calendar of Options

SEPTEMBER

*Weeks One and
Two of School*

PHASE	CONCERN
Anticipation	Self

- Schedule conference times for: clarifications/questions/problem solving around grouping issues, materials, and classroom management
- Apply the Planning Template (See Section 2: Structured Conversations: Maximizing Time and Attention) to a goal-setting conversation
- Collaborate on pre-assessment of student knowledge and skills and uses of data
- Establish a basic contact schedule for first month
- Begin work on Professional Portfolios*
- Send texts or emails or leave notes of encouragement in mail box

OCTOBER

PHASE	CONCERN
Survival	Self

- Collaborate on strategies for time management and planning upcoming instructional units
- Review teaching videos and discuss strategies/applications
- Facilitate a Beginning Teacher Support Group Meeting*
- Apply the Reflecting Template (See Section 2: Structured Conversations: Maximizing Time and Attention) for a learning-focused conversation on student progress
- Emphasize relationship building with students and create assessment tools to monitor

NOVEMBER

PHASE	CONCERN
Disillusionment	Task (Management)

- Create some Lively Lifelines*
- Encourage contact and activities with colleagues
- Discuss impact of student extracurricular activities
- Co-design formative assessments for student motivation
- Offer an Idea Bank of time and task management strategies
- Schedule a Problem Solving Partnership meeting*

DECEMBER

PHASE	CONCERN
Disillusionment	Task (Management)

- Acknowledge feelings of disillusionment and assist in determining priorities
- Analyze data on curricular implementation and student progress
- Use the Planning Template (See Section 2: Structured Conversations: Maximizing Time and Attention) to prepare for end-of-course exams, grades, and report cards
- Clarify goals for second semester
- Celebrate Success

Calendar of Options

JANUARY

PHASE	CONCERN
Rejuvenation	Impact

- Mutual sharing of professional growth goals and strategies
- Joint planning for upcoming units
- Clarify schedules, recordkeeping, reporting, etc.
- Encourage collaborative opportunities with other colleagues
- Attend a professional development offering
- Portfolio Interim Support Team Meeting

FEBRUARY

PHASE	CONCERN
Rejuvenation	Impact

- Create a video of your teaching; analyze with your beginning teacher
- Create a video in your beginning teacher's classroom; debrief
- Apply the Reflecting Template (See Section 2: Structured Conversations: Maximizing Time and Attention) to focus on student work products and progress
- Collaborate on an action research project
- Anticipate and share information regarding readiness for upcoming events (spring break, student testing, etc.)

MARCH

PHASE	CONCERN
Rejuvenation	Impact

- Reflect on a broad view of the curriculum to map progress; identify successes and challenges to date and anticipate upcoming units
- Continue to reflect on student performance data, explore cause-effect relationships, and strategize for different learning needs
- Check-in on readiness and any concerns regarding student files/records, parent conferences, test prep, etc.

APRIL

PHASE	CONCERN
Rejuvenation moving to Reflection	Impact

- Apply the Reflecting Template to assess progress on your beginning teacher's professional growth plan
- Anticipate and support emotional and logistical needs regarding spring student testing
- Clarify details regarding end-of-year schedules, final evaluations, field trips, etc.

Calendar of Options	

MAY	

PHASE	CONCERN
Reflection	Impact

- Apply the Reflecting Template (See Section 2: Structured Conversations: Maximizing Time and Attention) to identify insights, discoveries, patterns of learning for your beginning teacher
- Facilitate connection-making between personal learnings and application to future decisions
- Review student performance data and exploring cause-effect relationships
- Conduct a final check-in on end of year tasks, including record-keeping, reporting, parent communication, and required documentation

JUNE	

PHASE	CONCERN
Anticipation	Impact

- Share the load while Packing Up*
- Review the Professional Portfolio* or informal array of artifacts to explore significance, share learning and project goals for Year Two
- Celebrate successes

Awareness & Action:

Awareness:

Regarding the three functions: offering support, creating cognitive challenge, and facilitating professional vision:

1. What are your strength and stretch areas in each?
2. Where are your comfort zones, where would you like to develop increased confidence to produce a learning-focused balance between the three functions?

Action:

1. Schedule a conversation with your beginning teacher to discuss your mutual expectations, hopes, and concerns for your learning-focused relationship. Use the Mentoring Relationship Self-Assessment Rubric to focus the conversation (See Section 7: Downloadable Resources).
2. Given your reflections on relational needs and learning goals, use the Calendar of Options to select and/or generate phase appropriate strategies for success.

SECTION 2 | Structured Conversations: Maximizing Time and Attention

FOR ALL of us—mentors and beginning teachers alike—time may be our scarcest resource. In most cases, the challenge of developing and maintaining a learning-focused relationship exists outside of the expected activities and responsibilities of professional life. This chapter offers suggestions and strategies for time efficient, productive interactions between mentors and their colleagues. We begin with the most important use of time for learning-focused mentors: attending fully.

Attending Fully

Human beings are highly attuned to the nonverbal signals of others. This capacity for attunement has a biological basis. Attunement is the feeling that another person understands our experience and the reciprocal sense that this other person also feels understood. These feedback loops, or resonance circuits (Graham, 2010) develop in healthy parent-infant relationships, which establish the fundamental emotional and cognitive resources for positive relationships later in life. The capacity to send and perceive nonverbal communication is carried into adulthood. We communicate our intention and degree of attention to others by our posture, degree of muscle tension, and how we respond verbally and nonverbally. We fully join the conversation and the relationship by aligning our body with that of another. This behavior is especially important when the other person is ill-at-ease or when we are having difficulty understanding what is being said.

Ten minutes of our complete and focused attention is worth much more, in terms of maintaining a relationship and supporting learning, than thirty minutes with distractions. We actually maximize our time together by focusing our full attention on our beginning teacher.

While our capacity to attend fully is an innate part of being human, there are times when the potential for distraction or lack of attention is high. For example, when we are fatigued or stressed our mind might wander away from the present moment, and away from our colleague. When we have a great deal to do, with little time available, the same conditions apply. Given

Mirror Neurons: Aligning Brains

In the early 1990s neuroscientists Vittorio Gallese and Giacomo Rizzolatti at the University of Parma in Italy discovered a new class of neurons in the brains of macaques, a species of monkey. They named their discovery mirror neurons. These cells are active in the brain when a monkey performs a physical movement such as grasping or pointing. The most important finding was that the same cells—or mirror neurons—activate in the brains of other macaques that are observing these actions (Rizzolatti & Arbib, 1998). Mirror neurons were soon discovered in human brains as well. We mentally, physically, and emotionally join the action when we watch sporting events, or as the story unfolds in movies and plays.

the pressures of life in schools, conscious attention to being with our beginning teacher is a challenge that is particularly important to overcome. Being fully present is a powerful way to offer support.

Research indicates that the presence of phones blocks empathic connection. To have meaningful conversations, the presence of cell phones, even when turned off, can be problematic. Digital devices divide our attention between the person present and those in the outside world (Turkle, 2015). Although we are physically present, the world of constant connections distracts.

Communicating Our Attention

We signal our full attention nonverbally. Imagine you are in a restaurant, observing two people across the room. You can usually tell if they are relating well, even if you can't hear what they are saying. You might observe them leaning towards one another, nodding, smiling, and gesturing animatedly as they engage in conversation. When we give our full attention to others, we are in alignment.

Alignment has three distinct categories: physical, which includes muscle tension, posture, and gesture; vocal, which includes intonation, pace, and word choices; and breathing, which includes depth, duration, and rate. We align with others when several of these elements are matching. This connection usually occurs naturally when we are fully present. However, we can intentionally create alignment by purposefully matching our colleague's use of these nonverbal and verbal elements.

Being attuned is a manifestation of our full attention to another. When we are fully focused on our beginning teacher, attunement will be a natural part of the interaction. However, there are specific instances when we might pay particular attention to the use of behavioral elements in our interactions. These include times when we anticipate tension or anxiety or when tension or anxiety emerges within the conversation. For example, no matter how good the relationship between a mentor and beginning teacher, there is likely to be some anxiety when we engage in a reflecting conversation about a classroom observation. In addition, when preparing a beginning teacher for a potentially stressful event like parent-teacher conferences or a first classroom observation by the principal, it is an important time to consciously align.

Purposefully aligning is also useful when we are having difficulty understanding another person. Sometimes it feels like we're operating on different wavelengths. When miscommunication occurs, intentionally realigning and matching a colleague's nonverbal patterns is often an effective strategy. Another occasion for deliberate monitoring of alignment is when we, as a mentor, are having difficulty staying on track or our attention is diverted. So often, the limited time we have to meet with a beginning teacher is carved out from time we would devote to other tasks. Sometimes it is difficult to keep these tasks, both personal and professional, from distracting us. In this case, deliberate monitoring of alignment keeps our attention fully on our colleague.

> "Even a silent phone disconnects us."
> - Shari Turkle

ALIGNMENT CATEGORIES

Physical
- Muscle Tension
- Posture
- Gesture

Vocal
- Intonation
- Pace
- Word Choice

Breathing
- Depth
- Duration
- Rate

BE DELIBERATE WHEN / IF

- You anticipate tension or anxiety
- Tension or anxiety emerges
- You are having difficulty understanding another person
- You are distracted

Awareness & Action: Physical Alignment

Awareness:

1. What are some postural and gestural indicators you observe when people seem to be in alignment, or when they are not?

2. What are some effects for you, and for others, when you seem to be in alignment?

Action:

1. Watch the video on alignment, to observe reciprocity in action.

2. Anticipate some upcoming conversations and identify those in which focusing on alignment will be particularly important.

3. In a safe environment, for example with friends or family, intentionally experiment with matching and mismatching posture and gesture. Notice any differences.

Listening To Understand

Understanding the Habit Cycle: Distinguishing Habit from Choice

Physically aligning with the beginning teacher indicates our positive intention and enhances our ability to understand. Listening with total attention and with the intention to understand and not judge another is the foundational skill for mentors. In this way, we establish a safe environment for thinking together.

Maintaining this quality of listening presents both a mental and emotional challenge. There is a difference between understanding and agreement. Understanding means that we get another's perspective and ideas, but don't necessarily agree with them. Listening to understand requires that we control the chatter in our head. This is a discipline that can be learned. The human brain processes listening and speaking at significantly different rates, which creates a space for attention to wander (Atwater, 1992). Managing this discrepancy often requires developing new habits for mentors.

Physical Alignment Video
vimeo.com/miravia/alignment

Threat Detection: Creating Conditions for Cognitive Challenge

The human brain is wired for threat detection. We rapidly assess information in our environment for signs of danger. These signals, whether real or imagined, are fast tracked on the brain's neural superhighways, taking priority over other, more thoughtful processes. Incoming signals from visual, auditory, and tactile circuits flow into the amygdala, an almond shaped structure located deep within the limbic system within the midbrain. The amygdala's essential task is to connect emotional content to memory. Both positive and negative emotional experiences affect this neural chemistry. The cortex, which holds higher level thinking structures, has more circuits running from the amygdala than the reverse.

Biologically, emotions drive thinking and attention, helping us to create meaning. For conversations to be learning-focused the teacher has to feel safe not to know — thinking out loud is risk-taking. Perception of threat occurs when the teacher's amygdala makes a rapid assessment of the body language, facial expressions, voice tone, and language choices of the mentor. The molecules of emotion then hijack the brain/body system. The impression of threat inhibits thinking processes causing the teacher to shut down and revert to survival mode: freeze, fight, or flight.

Skilled mentors distinguish between habit and choice. Habits are neurological patterns that are reinforced by repetition. The way we listen is a habit. Habits are mentally and emotionally efficient, developed over years of practice. The listening patterns and purposes of social conversations are different from the listening patterns and purposes of mentoring conversations. It's important to explore whether a habit remains productive when contexts change. Charles Duhigg (2012) describes this behavioral pattern as the habit cycle (See Figure 2.1: The Habit Cycle), which includes a cue, an embedded routine, and some form of reward. Unquestioned habits are often the reason for tension and lack of productivity in learning-focused relationships. For example, telling without asking, fixing not teaching, or solving a problem instead of facilitating problem solving. Listening and responding patterns are prime examples of the ways the habit cycle operates in social and work settings.

Figure 2.1 The Habit Cycle

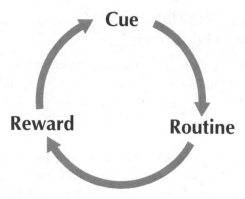

The Habit Cycle

A stimulus in the environment (cue) triggers a physical, mental, or emotional response (routine) which results in sense of satisfaction (reward). With repetition, this cycle becomes a habit.

All communication is based on how we listen. Four types of listening, in particular, stimulate the habit cycle. Each listening habit fires its own routine and reward. Listening drives our judgments, responses, and questions. When others speak, they cue our internal response habits and well-practiced routines kick-in. These routines pay off in the form of rewards that reinforce this cycle of reaction.

For example, some people relate through story. When they hear an anecdote or example told by a colleague, it triggers a memory search for a personal tale or experience to share. The reward is a feeling of connection to the other person and a sense of contribution to the conversation. In many social settings, this is an appropriate response. During mentoring conversations, this listening habit may impede focus and consume precious time. Four listening habits, or blocks to understanding are described below.

THE PRIMACY OF LISTENING

- Typical speaking rate: 150-180 words per minute

- Typical listening rate: 500-800 words per minute

"Nothing is stronger than habit."
   - Ovid

Blocks to Understanding

Individuals reared in Western culture develop the often counter-productive notion that one contributes to a conversation by speaking or interjecting. This expectation leads to conversations in which mentors are either talking or waiting to talk, but not listening to their colleagues. Not interrupting doesn't necessarily equate to listening. Often, silent individuals may have either mentally checked out or are composing their next remark.

To listen deeply, with full attention, requires energy and a commitment to the learning-focused relationship. Listening carefully to others also involves monitoring our own internal processes and developing awareness and control over several common internal distractions. These internal distractions or blocks to understanding shift our focus inward, to our own opinions, interests, judgments, and surety about potential solutions. This shift to self, or "I" listening, stimulates non-productive habits and distracts us from understanding others.

"I" Listening

Listening through the lenses of our own worldview diminishes our capacity to understand the perceptions and concerns of others. It is important for mentors to understand how their beginning teachers are thinking about their practice. There are four specific types of "I" listening: personal listening, detail listening, predictive listening, and certainty listening.

PERSONAL LISTENING
Personal listening is "me too" or "I would never" listening. It occurs when our minds shift from listening to understand others to considering what is being said with reference to our own experiences. In mentoring conversations, this "me too" listening stimulates anecdotes about the mentor's experiences with students, the content, or teaching practices. For example, "I had a student like that. . .", or "When I started teaching. . ." This storytelling consumes valuable meeting time. "I would never" listening triggers judgmental responses, cautions, or advice.

DETAIL LISTENING
Detail listening occurs when we focus our attention and inquiries on the specifics or minutia of the events or issues our beginning teacher is describing, rather than the thought processes related to these events. For example, our beginning teacher is planning a lesson requiring grouping students and providing hands on materials. We find ourselves wondering about the number and composition of students in each group. We then ask about these details, rather than the reasoning driving these decisions. This way of listening may be at the expense of the beginning teacher's learning. In addition, by listening for details and inquiring for the finer points we may be communicating doubt in our colleague's competence or knowledge about the topic at hand.

PREDICTIVE LISTENING
Predictive listening is listening *for* something, rather than *to* someone. This block occurs when we listen for what we expect to hear and filter out what is actually being said. Our biases influence these predictions, both negatively and positively. For example, generalizations about age, gender, ethnicity, attire, classroom organization, and our own belief system can unintentionally affect our expectations about the beginning teacher's character, competence, and professionalism. Predictive listening begins before anything is said and

"I" LISTENING

· Personal Listening

· Detail Listening

· Predictive Listening

· Certainty Listening

leads to selecting or rejecting from among the actual messages being expressed. This listening habit skews the conversation to a mentor driven focus rather than a beginning teacher driven focus.

CERTAINTY LISTENING

This listening block occurs when we are sure we know the solution to the problem, sometimes before we've listened enough to be sure that we understand the problem. This type of listening occurs when we prematurely stop attending outwardly and turn our attention to our own internal catalog of resources, viewpoints, and solutions. Even before a problem is fully framed and mutually understood, certainty listening leads to advice giving, either directly or disguised in the form of questions such as "have you tried. . . ?" or "have you thought about. . . ?"

Giving our full attention to a colleague contributes to relationship and to clear communication. These qualities are the foundations for mutual learning and future exploration. Awareness of our personal listening patterns is the first step in developing the capacity to attend fully. As awareness about full attention and our own listening prompts new routines, we develop new habits in our ways of attending and responding to our colleagues. These new habits further maximize our opportunities for learning by using shared and specific structures for guiding our interactions (See Figure 2.2: Breaking the Habit Cycle).

Figure 2.2 Breaking the Habit Cycle

Breaking the Habit Cycle

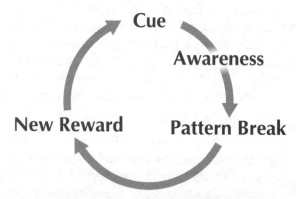

A stimulus in the environment (cue) flags consciousness about embedded routines (awareness); a new physical, mental, or emotional response replaces the old routine (pattern break); which results in the sense of satisfaction of building capacity in others (new reward), breaking the habit cycle.

Awareness & Action:

Awareness:

Complete the listening survey (See Section 7: Downloadable Resources):

1. What are some of your own listening tendencies?

2. What cues might trigger non-productive listening?

Action:

In low threat settings, such as a social occasion or a casual conversation, notice your automatic responses to the cues. Purposefully try out a new pattern. Notice the results for others and for you as a listener.

Structured Conversations

Applying an explicit structure to our conversations focuses attention, maximizes time efficiency, and provides a scaffold for stimulating and stretching thinking. For example, when a mentor and beginning teacher schedule planning time, a structure for guiding the conversation articulates essential categories to think about and ways of thinking about them, such as clarifying outcomes and identifying success criteria. Or, when a mentor and beginning teacher debrief a lesson, a structure for guiding the reflection articulates essential categories to think about and ways of thinking about them, such as searching for patterns and analyzing causes and effects. Structures help maintain forward movement and minimize side-tracks. In effective structured conversations, the mentor is the master of momentum and the beginning teacher is the keeper of the content.

The conversation templates that follow are samples of efficient guides for purposeful interactions. They are based on fundamental theories of learning (Marzano, 2007; Bransford, Brown, & Cocking, 1999) that suggest the importance of specific intentions within a learning-focused interaction. The templates on the following pages are based on the three phases in the Pathways Learning Model (Lipton & Wellman, 2000).

STRUCTURED
CONVERSATIONS

· Increase focus

· Increase time
  effectiveness

· Scaffold thinking
  processes

> *"In effective structured conversations, the mentor is the master of momentum and the beginning teacher is the keeper of the content."*

Each phase on the template serves a specific purpose. The Activating and Engaging phase builds relationship, stimulates mental and emotional awareness, and sets the scene for a thoughtful, learning-focused conversation. This phase establishes context and frames of reference by activating prior knowledge and experience, as well as surfacing the orientation and perception of the beginning teacher regarding the topic at hand. The Exploring and Discovering phase supports meaning-making and the construction of new knowledge and understanding. Whether in planning, reflecting, or problem solving this phase provides an opportunity for examining the details of specific results related to learning standards, making inferences, and analyzing experiences. The Organizing and Integrating phase shifts the conversation from a focus on a specific event to illuminating bigger ideas for transfer to future practice. The construction of generalizations and applications during this phase solidifies new learning and specifies next steps.

The three-phase conversation templates are tailored for specific purposes; planning, reflecting, and problem solving. Notice that these templates focus on specific cognitive outcomes in each phase. For example, when planning, the mentor's paraphrasing and inquiry supports the beginning teacher's predicting, designing, and choosing. While reflecting, the skillful mentor guides comparing, contrasting, cause-effect reasoning, pattern-seeking, and synthesis. Similarly, structured problem solving conversations produce thoughtful investigation, analysis, causal reasoning, and hypothesizing. These structures promote cognitive challenge and support transfer of these ways of thinking. Consistent application of the three-phase structure elevates the conversation from episodic to developmental thinking.

We propose the conversation templates as guidelines and not as recipes to be followed in a step-by-step fashion. These conversations usually begin with some way of inviting the beginning teacher to name what they'd most like to talk about. Asking the beginning teacher to weigh priorities is not only a respectful approach; it also provides a contextually sound view of the ways in which this novice is developing as a professional. By revealing the thinking that produces action, all learning-focused conversations are both acts of support and acts of assessment. The questions within each phase are intended as models and possibilities, not as a script.

Even with the templates in place, different conversations will take on different flavors depending on a variety of factors, including communication style preferences, cognitive and emotional readiness, time of year, and quality of relationship. These three templates apply the research on expert thinking and make it accessible to novices. Consistent use of these templates transfers that thinking to professional practice. When skillful mentors give thoughtful attention to their structured conversations, they produce powerful results.

Planning Conversations

Attention to planning and understanding the ways in which experts think about their plans are important to the development of novice teachers. Planning conversations model and reinforce the importance of goal-driven thinking. Effective teachers set clear goals for their instruction, and identify success criteria and specific systems for monitoring their achievement. They also anticipate potential problems and generate contingencies should their initial plan prove unsuccessful during implementation. Applying the template for planning helps internalize important planning arenas teachers must consider to produce learning environments and learning success for all of their students. Doing so with the support of a mentor increases a beginner's confidence and capacity for effective, independent instructional planning (See Figure 2.3: Learning-focused Conversations: A Template for Planning).

In the Activating and Engaging phase, establishing the context for the lesson or event allows the mentor and beginning teacher to get in the room together, both the immediate space of moment-to-moment alignment and the conceptual space of the beginning teacher's classroom. Experienced mentors preserve time for more elaborative thinking in the Exploring and Discovering phase by moving through this first phase as efficiently as possible. For example:

The beginning teacher might say:	The mentor might respond:
"I'm about to start a unit on local history. There are a lot of potential things I could put in."	*"So, you have some decisions about what to include. What are some of the major ideas and events you are considering?"*

Learning-focused Planning
Conversation Video
vimeo.com/miravia/planning

The second phase, Exploring and Discovering, is where the bulk of the time is spent in a typical planning conversation. The four focus arenas are arranged in order of priority. This is especially important to emphasize to novice teachers, who tend to spend more of their time designing activities and approaches, and less of their time clarifying goals, success indicators, and checks for understanding based on curriculum clarity and learning standards. Reducing activity-driven planning and increasing strategic approaches to student learning are important goals for increasing teaching expertise. For example:

The beginning teacher might say:	The mentor might respond:
"I'm hoping that my students will be able to see both the way things have changed and some ways they have stayed the same. And, how history continues to influence the community today."	*After a paraphrase: "Given those goals, what are some of the indicators of success you hope to see and hear in your students' work?"*

The third phase, Organizing and Integrating, concludes the conversation with specific next steps and personal learning goals that emerge from the conversation. The focus arenas in this phase of the template offer options for increasing awareness about connecting planning to high achievement and standards driven results. For example:

The beginning teacher might say:	The mentor might respond:
"I've got many ideas and some wonderful materials. My biggest concern is that I don't get carried away by my own enthusiasm and lose track of where the students are in the process."	*"With that awareness in mind, what are some of the things you need to most pay attention to in the early parts of the unit?"*

Each of these conversations illuminates areas of strength and potential stretch areas for beginning teachers. Skillful mentors select focusing questions and/or suggestions tailored to the learning needs of each of their beginning teachers.

Reflecting Conversations

Consistently reflecting upon and learning from practice is essential to growth throughout a professional career. Structured reflection with a mentor establishes that habit (See Figure 2.4: Learning-focused Conversations: A Template for Reflecting). These learning-focused conversations can occur after specific events such as lessons or meetings, or at scheduled intervals to reflect upon patterns of teaching practice and student learning. This process is especially useful at transition points in the curriculum, when unit topics switch, or at significant points in the school year, such as the close of marking periods.

In a reflecting conversation, the perceptions and perspectives of the beginning teacher are initially more important than your own impressions.

This orientation is true whether you were present for the event or not. If you have observed a lesson, this caution is especially important. Your comments, feedback, or suggestions for improvement all need a context in which to be heard. The context always initially belongs to the beginning teacher. It is, after all, her world and worldview you are entering.

Reflection is not about fixing what happened, but learning from it. The purpose of a reflecting conversation is to examine a lesson, unit, or other event to determine patterns, causes, and results that offer larger understandings about teaching and learning. Reflection is not a thinking skill. It is a selection of cognitive processes that influence perceptions and choices about future actions. Reflection is thinking backward to inform acting forward.

"Reflection is thinking backward
to inform acting forward."

In the Activating and Engaging phase, the mentor prompts the beginning teacher's recollections about the lesson or event. During this phase, skillful mentors listen for what their beginning teacher remembers and for what she may be missing, using data to support recollection. As expertise develops, teachers have more robust recall of lesson dynamics and details. Also during this phase, mentors invite their colleague to identify satisfactions and concerns and specific examples which will be carried forward for analysis during the Exploring and Discovering phase. In a reflecting conversation, skillful mentors note not just what their beginning teacher is recalling, but how they are thinking. These perspectives and perceptions frame the remainder of the conversation. For example:

The beginning teacher might say:	The mentor might respond:
"My introductory lesson got a bit convoluted. I think I had too many different ideas and concepts on the table at the same time."	*"So, given your recollections about the lesson, what might be a good starting point for our conversation?"*

The second phase, Exploring and Discovering, scaffolds explicit cognitive processes to construct learning from experience. During this phase, the thinking focuses on weighing priorities, seeking patterns, comparing and contrasting, and analyzing causes and effects. When reflecting, data inform perceptions and clarify understanding. Data also reveal gaps or gains between student performance and learning outcomes and teacher performance and professional standards. For example:

Learning-focused Reflecting
Conversation Video
vimeo.com/miravia/reflecting

The beginning teacher might say:	The mentor might respond:
"I was hoping that the students would start to see that some of the major organizers, such as where businesses are located and where roads run are mostly determined by the physical geography of the place, but I'm not sure that happened."	*"Those are major concepts for this age level. What are some comparisons between what you were hoping would happen and what you noticed in your students' responses?"*

During the Organizing and Integrating phase, skillful mentors widen the conversation from immediate issues to the bigger picture. Reflection is not about lesson-fixing, it is about distilling learning from processing specific experiences, generalizing new ways of thinking, and generating future applications. The generalizations, connection-making, applications, and personal learnings that emerge at this phase increase the likelihood of recognizing and applying new awareness and insight. This transfer is the true test of learning-focused conversations. Building habits of reflection and supporting transfer of and applications of learning is a critical skill for effective teachers and a key responsibility for mentors. For example:

The beginning teacher might say:	The mentor might respond:
"I'm starting to rethink this lesson and in fact, I'm going to redesign some of the upcoming lessons in the unit."	*"Based on what you're learning about lesson design, what are some of the guiding principles that might help you develop a stronger lesson focus?"*

Problem Solving Conversations

Teachers are continually confronted with problems to solve. Too often, beginning teachers do not have the tools or confidence to address them, and look to their mentors for solutions. A primary function of problem solving conversations is to develop effective and efficacious problem solvers. Hallmarks of an expert problem solver include the ability to envision desired outcomes and then strategize to achieve them. Skillful problem solvers can also articulate clear indicators of success. In a problem solving situation, problem framing is as important as solution generation. If you continually jump to advice giving, it can build dependency and can, over time, establish a one-up, one-down relationship. Problem finding and problem clarification are central features of expert thinking. Growth oriented mentors must remember to keep an eye on the bigger picture while responding to the issues and emotions of the present moment. The Problem Solving Template structures the conversation and develops and supports the thinking skills of effective problem solving (See Figure 2.5: Learning-focused Conversations: A Template for Problem Solving).

In the Activating and Engaging phase, the mentor seeks to understand the beginning teacher's concerns. The novice's perspective is the starting point for the conversation. The mentor listens to assess how the novice is viewing the issue, and pursues the conversation with this perspective in mind. For example:

The beginning teacher might say:	The mentor might respond:
"I'm not always sure which students are getting it at key points in the lesson."	*"So, you're looking for ways to more systematically check for understanding as a lesson progresses. Is this concern specific to this content area or does this occur in other areas as well?"*

During the Exploring and Discovering phase, the conversation shifts from the immediacy of the issue to the desired outcomes. This focus on the anticipated resolution releases the emotional energy needed for a productive problem solving conversation. Clarifying the indicators of success brings the solution into focus. Most important in this phase is to agree upon an operating theory for what might be causing the problem. Establishing three key pieces of information: clear outcomes, specific indicators of success, and a working theory of causation, creates the foundation for mentors and their beginning teachers to generate strategies and resources for solving the problem. For example:

The beginning teacher might say:	The mentor might respond:
"I'd really like to feel confident that I know what the kids are understanding at regular points in all my lessons."	*"So, you'd like to have a repertoire of formative assessment tools. Given that outcome what might be some indicators that tools you are using are making a difference?"*

During the Organizing and Integrating phase the beginning teacher identifies the necessary emotional and physical resources, and specific actions necessary for success. For example:

The beginning teacher might say:	The mentor might respond:
"I'm thinking that I need to learn how to build in some ways to monitor student learning into my lessons."	*After a paraphrase: "Based on that goal, what are some things you will do to get started?"*

As with all structured conversations, the specific instance—in this case a problem—is a vehicle for learning. Mindful mentors use problem solving conversation for two purposes. One purpose is that the conversation serves to solve the presenting problem. The second, and greater function, is to develop the problem solving skills of the beginning teacher.

Problem solving conversations can be scheduled or may arise spontaneously in hallway or faculty lounge "Gotta-minute?" moments. The Activating and Engaging phase takes on new light and new meaning in these conversations. Skilled mentors listen carefully to the presenting issues and concerns of the beginning teacher as well as to the perspectives and perceptions about the issues being described. Some problem solving conversations accomplish the bulk of the work in this phase. By paraphrasing, inquiring, reframing issues, and offering alternative frameworks, we model the habits of expert problem

Learning-focused Problem
Solving Conversation Video
vimeo.com/miravia/problemsolving

solvers who spend more time clarifying and defining the problem than do novices. Novice problem solvers often jump to solution thinking prematurely and spend time generating possible actions for ill-defined issues or concerns.

Once problems have been framed, the Exploring and Discovering phase proceeds very much like the planning conversation. Goals and success indicators are especially important to clarify. This process provides a reality check for the depth of the problem and for the qualities of possible best outcomes. Novices may need consultation during this phase, to identify choice points, generate options, and choose effective strategies.

Developing Fluency, Flexibility, and Focus

Navigating Within and Across the Conversation Templates

We offer a metaphor of map for the Conversation Templates. A map defines boundaries, clarifying what belongs inside and what is external to the territory. So, too, do these structures provide clarity about the parameters of the conversation. In this way, when used skillfully, they are especially time efficient, allowing either colleague to return to the agreed upon purpose(s) of the meeting. A map also can be shared, so both parties know what territory can be explored and what routes are possible—whether we take the same path each time, or vary it. Further, while each area on a map is clearly defined, we may choose to apportion our time visiting several neighborhoods, or spend most of it concentrated in one or two. In fact, once the mentor and beginning teacher have had some experience with the Conversation Templates, they are rarely applied linearly. That is, moving from one arena (establishing goals and outcomes) to another (potential choice points) and then to a third (indicators of success) and then back to the first (for more goals and outcomes) is quite common. It also frequently makes sense to navigate across the templates—drawing from past experiences, or reflecting, while developing a plan. Or finishing a reflecting conversation with questions for applying new learning to a future plan.

Balancing Support with Cognitive Challenge

As described above, the Planning, Reflecting, and Problem Solving Templates structure mentor-beginning teacher conversations. These guides enhance the efficiency of meeting time by providing a shared focus. They also serve as learning scaffolds, allowing novices to internalize the thinking protocols that guide experts when they plan, reflect, and problem solve.

The three forms of structured conversations exemplify expert ways of thinking about planning, reflecting, and problem solving. As a result, after several applications of the Conversation Templates, the beginning teacher comes to a meeting ready to respond to the challenging questions of the mentor. This readiness and confidence sets the stage for increasingly rigorous conversations about teaching and learning and increasingly effective approaches to the inevitable challenges of classroom life. Ultimately, the guiding questions embedded in these structures become the internal voice for novices when they are working independently.

Figure 2.3 Learning-Focused Conversations: A Template for Planning

Learning-focused Conversations: A Template for Planning

ACTIVATING AND ENGAGING

Establishing Context
- What are some things about your students' readiness (social skills, routines, self-management) that are influencing your lesson/unit design?
- What are some of the skills/knowledge students will need to bring to this lesson/unit to be successful?

Naming Presenting Issues
- What are some special areas/student needs you will need to address?
- What are some issues you anticipate might influence student learning?

EXPLORING AND DISCOVERING

Envisioning and Clarifying Goals and Outcomes
- As you think about what you know about your students, and the content, what are some key learning goals?
- What are some ways that these goals integrate with other content learning?
- What are some thinking/social skills students will need to apply?

Specifying Indicators of Success
- Given these goals, what are some things you expect to see/hear as students are achieving them?
- What are some formative assessments you're planning for monitoring student learning?
- What are some data sources you might use to determine student success?

Choosing Approaches, Strategies, and Resources
- What are some strategies you're planning that will both challenge students and support their success?
- What are some ways you'll ensure high engagement for all students?
- What are some resources or materials you/your students will need to support and extend student learning?

Determining Potential Choice Points and Concerns
- As you anticipate teaching the lesson/unit, what are some choice points that might arise?
- What are some options for supporting struggling students and enriching those who need greater challenge?
- Should there be a glitch in Plan A, what might be some options (Plan B)?

ORGANIZING AND INTEGRATING

Naming Personal Learning Opportunities
- What are some ways that this lesson/unit provides opportunities to pursue your own professional learning goals?
- As you anticipate teaching this lesson/unit, what are some opportunities for exercising new learning/skills?

Identifying Next Steps
- As a result of this conversation, what are some next steps?

Figure 2.4 Learning-Focused Conversations: A Template for Reflecting

Learning-focused Conversations: A Template for Reflecting

ACTIVATING AND ENGAGING

Recalling
- As you reflect on this lesson/unit, what are some things that come to mind?

Surfacing Perspectives and Perceptions
- In this lesson/unit, what was particularly satisfying?
- In this lesson/unit, what were some things that concerned you?

EXPLORING AND DISCOVERING

Weighing Priorities
- Given your impressions/recollections, what might we focus on that will be most useful to you?
- What are some examples (e.g., student responses, work samples, interaction patterns, observational notes) that stand out for you?

Searching for Patterns
- As you reflect on this lesson/unit, what are some patterns of which you are aware (e.g., student responses, time on task, student engagement)?
- Given what occurred how typical are these results?

Comparing and Contrasting
- Given the data, how similar or different is what you anticipated from what occurred (e.g., student responses, lesson pacing, student work products)?
- What are some comparisons you might make between your own effectiveness teaching this lesson as compared with previous practice (e.g., giving directions, responding to students, making adjustments)?

Analyzing Cause-Effect
- Given some of the results you're describing, what might be some factors that influenced what happened?
- What are some specific choices you made/actions you took that had the most positive effects?

ORGANIZING AND INTEGRATING

Making Generalizations
- What are some big ideas you're taking away from reflecting on this lesson/unit that will influence your future practice?
- Based on this experience, what are some new connections you're making (e.g., students, curriculum, instruction)?

Developing Applications
- As a result of new learning, what might be some adjustments you're considering for future lessons/ units?
- As a result of this conversation, what are some specific next steps?

Figure 2.5 Learning-Focused Conversations: A Template for Problem Solving

Learning-focused Conversations: A Template for Problem Solving

ACTIVATING AND ENGAGING

Describing Presenting Issues and Concerns

- What are some concerns you would like to discuss?
- If you were to give this issue a name, what might it be?

Investigating the Problem

- To what degree is this a stand alone issue or part of a larger pattern?
- On a scale of 1-5, what is your level of concern about this issue?

EXPLORING AND DISCOVERING

Envisioning and Clarifying Outcomes

- Given what you know about this problem, what would you most want to have happen once it is resolved?
- In contrast with the way you're feeling right now, how would you like to feel once this problem is resolved?
- Given your thinking at this point, what might be some possible outcomes?

Generating Indicators of Success

- Given your outcomes, what are some things you expect to see/hear as they are achieved?
- Given these outcomes, what are some ways you might measure/monitor progress?
- What might be some initial indicators that you're moving in the right direction?

Identifying Causation, Strategies, and Resources

- What are some causal factors you think might need to be addressed to resolve the problem?
- What are some strategies for developing the knowledge, skills, and attitudes necessary for success?
- What are some resources or materials you might draw upon to support your plan?

Anticipating Choice Points and Concerns

- As you anticipate implementing your plan, what might be some points of concern?
- Given your concerns, what might be some options should those occur?

ORGANIZING AND INTEGRATING

Establishing Personal Learning Strategies

- Given what you know about your own learning patterns, what are some strategies you'll use to keep your plan on track?
- How might you capture your learning from this situation to apply to future problems?

Naming Next Steps

- As a result of this conversation, what are some of your next steps?
- What is the first thing you'll need to do to get started?

Using Quick Forms

When the time, attention, or opportunity for a formal planning, reflecting, or problem solving conversation is not available, there are alternative options to facilitate a novice's thoughtful participation in learning-focused interactions. Practical and simply-structured protocols will save time and effectively balance support with cognitive challenge. Using these Quick Forms (See Section 7: Downloadable Resources) signals our expectations that, while we are very willing to provide support, we are not expecting to do all the thinking or problem solving for our beginning teacher. We consider these strategies to be scaffolds. That is, just as the construction metaphor suggests, they are structures to support a learner in reaching higher than they could without it. It also suggests that these scaffolds are temporary and adjustable, being moved where and when they are needed, and ultimately removed altogether. The three examples below require brief preparation prior to a scheduled meeting and can be applied in a variety of ways.

3 - 2 - 1

3 - 2 - 1 offers a structured approach for beginning teachers to organize thinking and focus communication. The information can be written on an index card or note pad. Or, if a beginning teacher is keeping a log or journal, the 3-2-1 structure offers an effective format for entries. Because it is so versatile, we use 3-2-1 for planning, reflecting, and problem solving. For example, prior to planning, ask a beginning teacher to jot down three possible goals for the lesson (or unit), two specific success indicators, and one strategy that might be used. Or, at the end of class, after teaching a new strategy, ask for three things that were noticed about the students' learning, two things that may have caused those results, and one new understanding or application. As a problem solving support, ask for three ways to think about the problem (or three perspectives on it), two potential contributing or causal factors, and one possible solution.

Asking a busy novice for six pieces of information makes the task doable while appropriately placing the responsibility for defining the problem or gathering the necessary information on the beginning teacher.

Stem Completions

Fill-ins, or stem completions, build confidence in responding to open-ended questions while honing a novice's thinking skills. Use the same stem completion regularly and consistently, for example, every Friday a beginning teacher might fill-in the following:

"The most interesting thing that happened this week was. . ." or, "One thing I'd never do the same way again is. . ." or, "This week, I was pleasantly surprised by. . ." or, "I discovered that. . ."

Or vary the stem to exercise and focus specific cognitive outcomes, such as comparison or pattern seeking. For example, "Some things that are the same about teaching reading and teaching math are. . ." Stem completions also serve to facilitate professional vision. Generate stems that require articulation of values. For example, "The most important thing a teacher can do for struggling students is. . ." or, "A priority for me as a learning-focused teacher is. . ."

Stem completions support and challenge thinking and provide a quick start for purposeful mentor-beginning teacher interactions. They also develop the important habits of reflective, value-driven professional practice.

P + M - I*

The P + M - I*, or Plus, Minus, Interesting Frame, developed by Edward DeBono, supports reflection, self-assessment, and evaluative thinking. A three-column sheet is used to record the Pluses, or positive aspects, of an event, plan or situation; the Minuses, or negative aspects; and the Interesting or intriguing ideas that are neither plus nor minus. For example, a new teacher might do a P + M - I* on a solution he or she is considering, or for a plan to try a new classroom management system. The P + M - I* can be used to reflect upon a unit that was just completed or a recently conducted parent conference.

When You Can't Meet Face-to-Face

There are times when it is difficult for mentors and beginning teachers to schedule meeting time. However, this obstacle doesn't eliminate the need for ongoing communication. We can maintain communication using some traditional and some novel methods to keep in touch. Of course, communicating by telephone, text, Skype, or e-mail are ways to touch base without a formal meeting. To enhance these methods, get in the habit of using Quick Forms, like the 3-2-1, stem completions, P + M - I* or other structures to facilitate clear, concise communication while exercising the important thinking skills these structures require.

In addition to those described above, use the following Quick Forms (See Section 7: Downloadable Resources) for enhancing mentor-beginning teacher communication when meeting is not possible or must be delayed.

DOUBLE ENTRY JOURNALS

Taking a page from classroom-based literacy strategies, Double Entry Journals also work well for mentors and beginning teachers. The beginning teacher enters a dated entry in the left-hand column; the mentor responds in the right-hand column and returns the journal to the beginning teacher. This simple exchange can be done digitally to provide a quick tip in a timely fashion, increase a novice's confidence in a choice or decision, or offer the emotional support of knowing someone is connected and listening.

QUESTIONS OF THE WEEK

A variation on the Double Entry Journal, the Questions of the Week has a similar format. That is, two columns are used: the left-hand columns are labeled by days of the week, the right-hand column is for the mentor's response. The Questions of the Week strategy offers the novice a chance to ask a question at the end of each day, or on days when questions arise, and send them to their mentor. In many cases, the mentor then offers a quick response or resource or, if necessary, suggests a longer communication or face-to-face meeting.

The process can also be reversed, with the mentor filling the left-hand column and offering the beginning teacher a question to ponder.

The time frames for this strategy can be modified in many ways. For example, a Question of the Week could be a Friday ritual with the beginning teacher looking forward to a response on Monday morning; or, change to Questions of the Month or Marking Period, and so on.

MINDFUL MEMORANDUM

The Mindful Memorandum has a priority gauge that directs the mentor's attention to the beginning teacher's level of need: Need to talk now!; When you can, but soon; or Whenever. In addition, it requires concise, organized communication on whether the topic is an urgent problem or an interesting anecdote.

Awareness & Action: Applying the Conversation Templates

Awareness:

1. Where do you tend to focus your energy in a planning conversation? What keeps you focused; what takes you off-track?

2. Where do you tend to focus your energy in a reflecting conversation? What keeps you focused; what takes you off-track?

3. Where do you tend to focus your energy in a problem solving conversation? What keeps you focused; what takes you off-track?

Action:

1. Send the relevant template in advance to your beginning teacher.

2. Review the conversation templates prior to meeting with your beginning teacher.

3. Keep a copy of the conversation template visible during your learning-focused conversation.

SECTION 3 | Learning-Focused Conversations: A Continuum of Interaction

Skilled mentors support novices in learning from experience, helping them to align future action with emerging insights. Being clear about intention as a growth agent and acting congruently creates a climate for thinking, risk-taking, and problem solving. Attending to the relationship is critical to maintaining the emotional safety necessary for learning.

When communicating, our outer cues, including intonation, gesture, facial expressions, posture, and muscle tension reflect our inner processes. These indicators, as well as specific things a colleague might say, provide a feedback loop for determining an effective mentoring stance and flexibly applying the learning-focused toolkit. When mentors embrace the intention to promote growth, they focus their full attention on these signals from their beginning teacher and adjust their actions accordingly (See Figure 3.1: Intention-Driven Action).

Just as classroom teachers monitor and adjust to meet the needs of their learners, attentive mentors respond to the developmental readiness of their beginning teachers. They do so by balancing cognitive challenge and offering support, adjusting the ratio of information and inquiry in their learning-focused conversations.

Figure 3.1 Intention-Driven Action

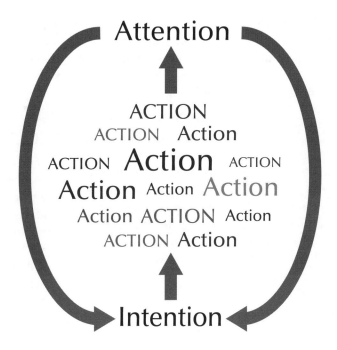

Four Stances: The Continuum of Learning-focused Interaction

Skilled mentors navigate across a Continuum of Interaction to offer support, create cognitive challenge, and facilitate professional vision. Within learning-focused conversations, they flex between four stances: calibrating, consulting, collaborating, and coaching to develop their beginning teacher's ability to reflect upon practice, generate ideas, make more effective choices, and increase professional expertise. In standards-driven systems, conversations between mentors and their beginning teachers explore the connections between present practices and expected results. Whether the mentor or beginning teacher provides the information, analysis, or goals determines the stance. In the calibrating stance, the mentor performs this function, in a collaborating stance, both parties define the fit, and from a coaching stance, the beginning teacher self-assesses. The ultimate aims of these interactions are to support a beginning teacher's capacities to self-monitor, self-manage, and self-modify with increasing confidence and skill.

Versatility across the Continuum provides response patterns that are developmentally and contextually appropriate for meeting the learning needs of novices. Facility with the Continuum is also a developmental process for mentors. With deliberate application, mentors develop through three levels of use: fluency of interaction, flexibility of interaction, and fluidity of interaction.

Fluency of interaction: Fluent mentors are clear about the definition and purpose of each of the four stances. Verbal and nonverbal cues from the beginning teacher inform the choice of stance and when to shift stances. Having a repertoire of strategies for each stance increases a mentor's ability to make the most effective choice of stance.

Flexibility of interaction: Flexible mentors differentiate conversations by responding to the teacher's immediate emotional and cognitive needs, keeping in mind the ultimate goal of development over time. These mentors apply clear criteria for when and why to choose a specific stance at a specific time in a learning-focused conversation.

NAVIGATING THE CONTINUUM OF INTERACTION

Three levels of use:
- Fluency
- Flexibility
- Fluidity

CALIBRATE from the Greek Kalapous, meaning wooden foot, in modern days this term describes a shoemaker's last. Taking this stance means that the mentor will determine and describe the fit between the beginning teacher's practice and the expected standard of performance.	CONSULT from the Latin consultare, meaning to give or take counsel. This approach moves beyond simple advice giving. To offer counsel as a mentor is to provide the why, what, and how of your thinking.	COLLABORATE from the Latin collaborare, meaning to work together. As a mentor, this exchange means creating a space for true, shared idea generation and reflection with attention to one's own impulse control, so the new teacher has room and an invitation to fully participate as an equal.	COACH from the French coche, the German and kutsche, the Hungarian, kocsi, after Kocs, a town in Hungary where fine carriages were built. A mentor as a coach is a vehicle for transporting a valued colleague from one place to another. It is the beginning teacher's journey. The mentor/coach is a guide and support system.

Fluidity of interaction: Fluid mentors have a level of automaticity that supports their ability to attend and respond to complexities and nuances, drawing upon a wide repertoire of knowledge and skills to make the match that produces the most learning in the moment. Skillful mentors apply the Continuum seamlessly, shifting stances as needed.

Figure 3.2 Continuum of Learning-focused Interaction

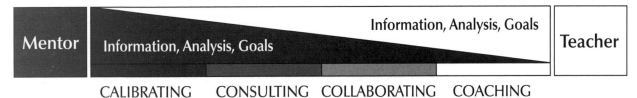

These capacities build upon one another along a developmental pathway. Fluent mentors become increasingly more flexible, expanding their skill sets to differentiate conversations, monitoring goals for teachers' development over time. Mentors who operate fluidly have a more refined and integrated skill set. These mentors are able to pay attention at multiple levels to make choices and construct responses with increased efficiency and effectiveness.

Increasing Capacity, Decreasing Dependency

The mentor's primary goal is to increase beginning teachers' capacities to learn from their teaching, while decreasing dependency on the mentor. Expert teachers envision, monitor, and reflect upon student learning outcomes, their own professional learning goals, and potential problems or gaps.

In any learning-focused conversation there is a flow of information, analysis, insights, and goals. Mentors, beginning teachers, or both can generate these elements. These areas of focus emerge in learning-focused conversations in several ways. The source of these elements defines the stance at any given point in the conversation. At times it may be most appropriate to calibrate; that is, the mentor clarifies learning and teaching standards in connection to present practice. In this stance, the mentor uses data to reinforce expectations, set goals, and name next steps. At other points, to consult may be the better fit; that is, the mentor is the source of counsel and advice about processes, protocols, choices, and actions. The mentor as consultant draws upon her own repertoire, experiences, and expertise to advocate and offer perspectives and options. Alternatively, it may be most effective for mentors to collaborate; that is, co-generate ideas while planning, reflecting, and problem solving. In this stance, the mentor and beginning teacher share the work of idea generation, data analysis, problem framing, and goal setting. At other times to coach is the most productive option. The mentor inquires to stimulate and stretch the beginning teacher's thinking and strengthen her decision making skills.

These four stances work in concert to balance information with the opportunity for the new teacher to process and apply it. A common misconception is a comparison between navigating the Continuum of Interaction and the Gradual Release of Responsibility (GRR) model of teaching. The GRR approach is an "I do it, we do it, you do it" (Fisher & Frey, 2007) and assumes the need for the teacher to provide the initial information and gradually, as learners gain more skill and knowledge, shift the percentage of input to be more student-driven. This approach explicitly moves in one direction toward greater self-reliance, intervening with "I do it", or even "we do it" when something is not working. In contrast, while the goal of increasing self-reliance is similar, the Continuum of Interaction does not flow directionally, but is a tool for balancing responsibility for providing and constructing information. In this model, shifting to a consulting stance can have great value in producing learning.

Beginning teachers learn when they are able to take information and apply it to their own setting. Segmenting ideas and checks for understanding reduce the potential for information overload. Skilled mentors shift stances to balance information with inquiry based on the beginning perspectives and readiness. For example, using a consult to coach pattern by offering information and then inquiring about applications for the beginning teacher's practice encourages transfer of ideas. Based on the developmental readiness of the new teacher, mindful mentors shape their responses to scaffold and stretch thinking. A mindful mentor would never have a conversation that is 100% in a consulting stance, but might have a conversation that is 100% in a coaching stance. By listening and paraphrasing to understand without judgment, mentors consider options for response based on the four stances. Versatility with, and intentional use of, all four stances are essential resources for customizing interactions. For example:

A shift from Consulting (offering information as a principle of practice) to Collaborating:
"Behavioral interventions require patience, tenacity, and consistency to be effective. Given all the potential distractors, let's generate some strategies you might use to ensure effective application."

A shift from Consulting (offering ideas as a menu) to Coaching:
"It's important to check for understanding before transitioning to another topic. There are a number of effective ways to do that; you might ask for a hand signal, you might collect exit slips about the content, or call on students randomly to provide a correct answer. Given what you know about your kids, which might work best?"

A shift from Collaborating to Consulting:
"So, we've generated some pros and cons for several methods to get students' attention. Given that the pros for using signals seems more robust, I would suggest that you select one to start with and be sure to use it consistently, which will establish a routine and reinforce expectations."

A shift from Coaching to Calibrating:
After an inquiry and the new teacher's response, the mentor replies:
"So, as you review your formative data, you seem unsure about your students' skills related to grade level writing standards. Take a look at the exemplar for supporting the main idea in expository writing, compared to these writing samples. It appears that 40% percent of your students are meeting proficiency standards in this strand."

CALIBRATING VS. CALIBRATION

Calibration

- Is necessary in any standards-driven conversation

- Aligns performance to standards

- Can occur in the calibrating, collaborating, or coaching stances

Calibrating

- Who does the calibration defines the stance

- In the calibrating stance, the mentor serves this function

- In the collaborating stance, calibration is co-generated

- In the coaching stance, the teacher does the calibration

Calibrating

The intention of the calibrating stance is to ensure alignment between classroom practice and expected teaching and learning standards. Although mentors are not evaluators, they emphasize the importance of teaching and learning standards as the drivers of practice. When calibrating, the mentor clarifies the standards using data to highlight both gaps and gains.

The calibrating stance is necessary when a beginning teacher is unable to analyze her own practice and identify the fit between current performance and expected standards. In the calibrating stance, the mentor provides data and highlights exemplary practices to motivate stretch goals and facilitate professional vision.

In this case, the guiding question for the mentor when considering a calibrating stance is:
"Given teaching and learning standards and present performance, what do the data indicate as growth areas for this teacher?"

FUNCTION OF THE CALIBRATING STANCE

In the calibrating stance, the mentor clarifies standards to be sure they are well understood by the beginning teacher and uses data to identify gaps and gains. The calibrating mentor also references both standards and data to highlight achievements and identify problems. In this stance it is the mentor who names goals and related actions and outcomes.

CAUTIONS WHEN CALIBRATING

Given the pressing needs of beginning teachers, it is often challenging to maintain a growth orientation. For mentors, there is constant choice-making about where to focus energy and attention, and how much information to provide while embracing a developmental approach. It is essential that any judgments are supported by clear, external criteria and standards. The use of literal data, such as observation notes, student work products, lesson plans, and classroom artifacts is critical to avoid subjectivity or bias. When calibrating, mentors must not let personal preferences becomes prescriptions.

The calibrating and consulting stances are closely related. Each provides information and is more mentor-driven. For this reason, each is a launch point for moving to collaborating or coaching. In the calibrating stance, the mentor articulates necessary outcomes and actions. In the consulting stance, the mentor shares why these outcomes are important and provides options for ways to achieve them.

Consulting

The intention of the consulting stance is to offer support by providing information about policies and procedures, learning and learners, curriculum and content, and standards and effective practices that may not be presently available to the beginning teacher. The consulting mentor shares information in two important categories: information about how the district and school operate, and information about teaching and learning.

The first category includes the procedural expectations of the district and school, including legal and policy guidelines for matters like discipline and special education. In the consulting stance, the mentor might share information about policies for getting approval for, and conducting field trips, and how to manage bureaucratic tasks such as completing personnel forms and ordering materials.

The second category includes information about the craft of teaching including such things as: establishing a safe and equitable classroom climate, developing a repertoire of instructional strategies, and formative assessments to guide thoughtful curriculum implementation. This information offers beginning teachers opportunities for making informed choices and decisions as they apply these ideas and suggestions in their classrooms.

So, for mentors, a guiding question when considering a consulting stance is: *What information, ideas, and technical resources might be most useful for me to offer this teacher, at this time?*

FUNCTION OF THE CONSULTING STANCE

In the consulting stance, the mentor contextualizes standards by offering specific examples to ensure that the beginning teacher understands expectations as they apply to her own classroom. The consulting mentor uses data to interpret present results, naming possible causes and possible approaches for continuous improvement. Given this analysis of gaps or gains, a thoughtful mentor shares relevant information about learning and learners and curriculum and content. When consulting, a mentor might also offer alternative ways to think about a presenting issue or concern (See Table 3.1: Mentor Moves When Consulting).

By offering, "Here is what you should pay attention to" and "Here is why that matters" and "Here are some options", learning-focused mentors make their thinking transparent. As beginning teachers internalize principles of learning and teaching, these understandings become resources for generating their own approaches and solutions.

In planning for action, skillful mentors propose possible teacher goals to promote student achievement and professional growth, and provide opportunities for the teacher to choose and prioritize. Clarifying indicators of success and recommending timelines for completion are essential parts of the process.

CAUTIONS WHEN CONSULTING

The verb to consult comes from the Latin consultare meaning to give or take counsel. It is important to distinguish learning-focused consultation from simply fixing or telling. For many mentors, the pressing needs they observe in classrooms or working with an anxious novice triggers the impulse to help, by providing solutions, or offering advice. While in the short term this inclination may reduce the burdens of novice teachers or temporarily resolve an urgent issue, context-rich learning opportunities may be missed if fixing or saving is the prevalent form of response. Further, advice without explanation of the underlying choice points and guiding principles rarely develops teachers' abilities to transfer learning to new settings or to generate solutions on their own.

Mindful mentors need to be aware of their own patterns when applying the Continuum of Interaction. If overused, the consulting stance builds dependency on the mentor for problem solving. Consultation that is learning-focused within a professional relationship offers the teacher both immediate support

"What do you think I should do about. . . ? is the cheddar on the mousetrap."
- Michael Bungay Stanier

and the resources for tackling future problems with increasing independence whatever the teacher's level of performance. Learning-focused mentors do not allow their personal passion or organizational pressures to overcome patience with a beginning teacher's developmental process.

Table 3.1 Mentor Moves When Consulting

Mentor Move	What is it?	Might look/sound like
Offer a menu	If one idea is useful, several are even more effective. Suggesting multiple options when planning or problem solving (we suggest at least three) provides information and support while leaving the choice making, and the responsibility for making that choice with the beginning teacher.	*"Given your concerns about developing meaningful homework assignments, here are three options to consider. . ."* *"Given your goal to help your students think deeply about both content and learning processes some ways to provide thinking time might include: 1) Pausing for 3-5 seconds after inquiring or offering a prompt 2) Use a Think-Pair-Share protocol 3) Add a writing step and have them Think-Write on their own before Pairing and Sharing."*
Think aloud	When a mentor connects a specific strategy to the broader principles of best practice, the new teacher learns to apply the principle as well as the individual idea. When a mentor shares the thinking process that leads to a solution, the new teacher benefits from a deeper understanding of the process of problem solving. Just as important, thinking aloud debunks the myth that experienced teachers have all the answers and no longer struggle with the complexity of decision making.	*"When I encounter situations like this, I first search for. . . Then I ask myself. . . So, in this case, you might look for. . ."* *"When I consider ways to improve the efficiency of transition times in the classroom my goals are to preserve student learning time and enlist the students help in moving smoothly from task-to-task or large group to small group activities. I've learned that sharing these goals with the class makes a difference so that when I use musical timing strategies or a beat the clock type of system they know what the outcomes are and why this matters."*
Share what, why, how	When sharing expertise, an effective verbal pattern is describing the what, why, and how of an idea or suggestion. This consulting move relates the what and how of possible actions to the underlying principles of practice that are the drivers of these choices. As beginning teachers come to better understand these principles they are more able to generate their own ideas and strategies.	*"Here is a strategy for addressing that issue (what); which is likely to be effective because (why); and this is how you might apply it (how)."* *(What) "Given your concerns about behavioral conflicts during small group work, let me offer a strategy for addressing these issues." (Why) "Student engagement in the problem solving process increases their ownership of both the problem and the solution. While this initially takes some time, it saves time in the long run." (How) "One way to do this is to have students individually write down what they think is causing the friction with others and then name three possible solutions. Then have the students share these with one another and develop a shared definition of the problem, and then select the most appropriate solution."*

Table 3.1 Mentor Moves When Consulting *(continued)*

Mentor Move	What is it?	Might look/sound like
Refer to research	Referring to specific research-based best practices is often a productive consultation strategy. This approach offers expert advice drawn from credible sources that can be applied to the current situation.	*"Based on your questions and concerns, the research related to these indicates that. . ."* *"The research on having students create graphic representations has been very consistent across grade levels and content areas. One application of those ideas to consider here would be to teach your students how to develop cause and effect diagrams to illustrate the important relationships in this history lesson."*
State a principle of practice	Connecting a specific strategy or solution to the broader principles of effective practice provides an opportunity to learn and apply the principle, as well as the individual ideas, in other situations. As beginning teachers internalize the big ideas represented by principles of practice they are increasingly able to generate or search for strategies that match these organizers.	*"An important principle of practice related to (topic) is _____; so a strategy like (suggestion) should be effective in this situation."* *"Stating expectations clearly and reinforcing them through both repetition and highlighting examples of when students are meeting them is an important part of both managing student behavior and developing a supportive classroom learning environment. Some ways to do this are to create a chart stating your goals and for each lesson in the first weeks of school asking students what they will see and hear during the lesson as indicators of success in meeting these goals."*
Generate categories	Ideas or solutions as categories provide a wider range of choice and a richer opportunity for learning than discrete strategies or applications. For example, a category such as grouping students is broader than putting students in pairs or suggesting a specific partnering strategy. This approach is especially effective when categories are offered as a menu.	*"Many classroom and instructional issues involve multiple categories of thinking and planning. In this case you need to consider. . . and. . . and. . ."* *"Several broad categories of successful classroom management include attention moves, establishing routines, maintaining momentum, and developing effective transitions between activities."*
Name causal factors	Rather than suggesting potential solutions, it can be very productive to offer several factors that might be producing the problem. This consulting move models the analytical habits of more expert teachers, who search for learning gaps or behavioral causes that might be producing any observable behaviors about which they have concerns.	*"There are several things that typically would produce that behavior (or result); for example, _____, _____ or _____."* *"Regarding your goal to get your students to engage more thoroughly in your lessons, some factors that typically drive this are: 1) helping students access prior knowledge – both from previous lessons and their own lives 2) being sure there are appropriate scaffolds for the tasks you assign, and 3) frequent and varied checks for understanding to see who's getting it and who needs more support at that point in time."*

Table 3.1 Mentor Moves When Consulting *(continued)*

Mentor Move	What is it?	Might look/sound like
Consider an alternative point of view	Novices tend to have limited viewpoints for examining the issues and concerns that arise in their practice. When a novice is only seeing things one-way, mentors stimulate effective problem solving by offering multiple perspectives. For example, offering thoughts on how others such as parents, students, colleagues, or administrators might consider the issue.	*"You seem to be viewing this situation from the perspective of. . . Some other perspectives to consider are. . . and. . ."* *"It is possible that your students are not perceiving the purposes of the new reward system in the ways that you had intended. It might be that your students have a different idea about what is rewarding."*
Reframe the problem or issue	Expert problem solvers spend a greater amount of time defining a problem than they do strategizing solutions. Novel approaches to the problem definition not only release new energy and ideas, but often lead to a more effective solution. Related to considering alternative perspectives, reframing is changing the context or representation of a problem; including positive or useful aspects of the issue and alternative descriptions of the goal or approach to the problem.	*"You appear to be framing this issue as one in which. . ."* *"Another way to think about it is. . ."* *"There are several ways to think about classroom climate and culture. Typically, teachers search for simple rules and fair consequences to apply equally. Another approach is to work from the inside out and support students in developing the self-management skills to be productive classroom citizens and contributing group members."*

Collaborating

The intention of the collaborating stance is to scaffold cognitive challenge by contributing to and stimulating the information flow. Mentors create this opportunity by opening a space for co-generation of ideas and co-construction of plans. In this stance, mindful mentors model collaborative processes and exercise the important professional skill of collegial interaction.

So, for mentors, a guiding question for the collaborating stance is:
What are some ways to balance my contributions with this teacher's knowledge and experience?

FUNCTION OF THE COLLABORATING STANCE

Collaborative interactions involve shared analysis, problem solving, decision-making, and reflection. The reciprocal nature of collaboration supports mutual learning, mutual growth, and mutual respect. Each party participates, alternately listening, paraphrasing, and inquiring to develop shared understandings and productive outcomes. In this stance, mentors and beginning teachers jointly calibrate teaching and learning performance to the standards. They use data to analyze gaps and gains and generate actions and goals appropriate to the beginning teacher's development and context. Ideas emerge through brainstorming, elaboration, and exploration of external resources (See Table 3.2: Mentor Moves When Collaborating).

A mentor's careful pausing and paraphrasing opens up the emotional and thinking space in which this stance flourishes. The use of inclusive pronouns, such as us, our, and we or we're invites the beginning teacher to join in.

After paraphrasing, "so we have a list of seven items to think about...," the mentor can then shift to coaching or consulting based on her sense of which stance might be most appropriate.

CAUTIONS WHEN COLLABORATING

Adopting a collaborative stance signals respect and the expectation of a collegial relationship. It is important to resist impulsivity and jump in and do the bulk of the analysis and thinking. Mindful mentors monitor for balance in idea production and do not allow their own personal enthusiasm and preferences to override the intention to co-create.

Table 3.2 Mentor Moves When Collaborating

Mentor Move	What is it?	Might look/sound like
Participate in a brainstorming session	Mutual generation of information is the most fundamental collaborative action. The nonjudgmental quality of brainstorming keeps the exchange reciprocal. Generate possible reasons or causes for a particular circumstance or event, a variety of ideas or strategies, potential solutions to a presenting problem or interventions that might be productive for an individual or group of students.	*"So, there are some students who seem to get distracted easily during class discussions. Let's brainstorm some reasons why that might be happening."* *"Let's look at each of the possible attention moves you're considering and generate a list of pros and cons for each."*
Engage in co-planning/ co-teaching	Working together to create a lesson or a unit of study, and extending that activity by teaching together are natural expressions of a collaborative relationship. As learning-focused mentors, however, we must be sure to include the beginning teacher fully in the process, creating a true collaboration.	*"Let's think about the key outcomes for this lesson, and which kids might need some special attention. What's your sense of that?"* *"As we review the plan, let's identify who'll take the lead on which parts. Where would you like to start?"*
Become study buddies	A mentor and new teacher might become Study Buddies, choosing to learn together about a new instructional methodology or reading current articles on classroom related research. This common focus provides a launching point for creating new ideas and trying new strategies. The learning aspect is deepened when we identify and share feedback about our mutual experimentation and set new goals for learning and sharing.	*"Given your professional goal of more ways to check for understanding, how about we explore some current resources, choose a few strategies and both experiment with them. Then we can compare notes at our next meeting."*

Table 3.2 Mentor Moves When Collaborating *(continued)*

Mentor Move	What is it?	Might look/sound like
Design and conduct action research	Extending a Study Buddy relationship into a more formal action research project deepens the learning potential and encourages a spirit of conscious curiosity about our practice. In addition, instilling a norm of experimentation early in a novice's career is a powerful way to facilitate a professional vision as a life-long learner.	*"So, in thinking about students' writing skills you're curious about how to improve word choice in creative pieces. Let's explore a few current approaches for building vocabulary and written expression and design a systematic way to see which ones are most effective for our students."*
Explore case studies	Case studies provide a context for dialogue about practice. The open-ended nature of most cases offers an opportunity to consider the complexities of teaching. Exploring a case study from a collaborative stance can be an intriguing learning experience for both partners.	*"We can explore a few case studies that offer issues similar to the one you're experiencing with the conflicts in your classroom. That will give us a focus for looking for causes, considering approaches, and maybe choosing some next steps."*

Coaching

In the Continuum of Learning-focused Interaction, a coaching stance is synonymous with inquiring. The intention of the coaching stance is to influence the internal dialogue of the beginning teacher to stimulate increasingly expert ways of thinking about practice. This stance is to support a colleague's thinking, problem solving, and goal clarification. Our thinking about this stance emerges from the work of Arthur Costa and Robert Garmston (2016).

The guiding question for mentors using a coaching stance is:
"What inquiries might stimulate and stretch this teacher's thinking at this time."

FUNCTION OF THE COACHING STANCE

In a coaching stance, the mentor uses standards and data as focal points for crafting inquiries about gaps and gains, and supports the beginning teacher's idea production by inquiring, paraphrasing, pausing, and probing for details.

In this stance, beginning teachers calibrate their own teaching and learning performance to the standards. Mindful mentors use questions to stimulate thinking about results, patterns, and causal factors for classroom outcomes. These inquiries are not focused solely on the Whats and Hows of planned actions or past events. They also focus on the Whys of choices, possibilities, and connections. The intention is to continually enlarge the context as the new teacher's professional confidence increases. For example, initially the focus might be on establishing productive classroom routines and ultimately move to building an inclusive culture for learning.

Mindful mentors emphasize the importance of problem framing as an essential resource for pursuing continued improvement. The ultimate aim of this stance is to develop the internal resources of self-coaching. Over time, the patterns of a mentor's inquiry within templates for planning, reflecting, and problem solving transfer to the beginning teacher's inner voice so she can be guided by this professional self-talk.

CAUTIONS WHEN COACHING

The word coach describes a form of conveyance that transports someone from where they are to where they would like to go. In the same way, when the mentor applies a coaching stance, she is attuned to the goals of the beginning teacher. However, inquiries can cause embarrassment or frustration when there is a lack of knowledge or experience. It is important to know when to navigate from this stance to provide information or direction and then return to inquiry when potential options and actions are available. Questions should stimulate and stretch, not strain. Keep in mind, that if you have a preferred response, don't ask a question—shift to a consulting stance instead. Productive inquiries allow for multiple responses.

CUEING STANCE NON-VERBALLY

Nonverbal tools, such as posture, gesture, and voice tone are all subtle indicators of the stance we are taking.

In the calibrating and consulting stances, the posture tends to be a bit more upright, leaning back slightly from the conversation. The mentor's voice tends to be less rhythmic and more credible with a narrower range of modulation than the coaching voice. This is the posture and voice of experience and wisdom. In a calibrating stance, neutral pronouns prevail, for example, the data, these students, this work sample. However, in the consulting stance, the mentor often uses the pronouns I or my as in, "Here's how I think about issues like that" or "from my perspective it seems. . ."

In a collaborating stance, the posture is metaphorically and often physically side-by-side. The voice tone is collegial, approvingly confident, with a blend of we and you pronoun types.

In a coaching stance, there is greater eye contact, closer proximity, leaning in, and more rhythmic speech patterns. The voice is approachable and invitational. This is the posture and voice of inquiry, creating a psychologically safe space for thinking and reflecting. The dominant pronoun is you, as in "So, you're noticing some patterns in your classroom that seem to be working" or "What are some comparisons you might make between those students who are succeeding with this learning objective and those who are struggling?"

Navigating the Continuum of Interaction

Expert mentors listen for and note the ways in which beginning teachers describe and interpret the actions and outcomes in their classrooms, and the ways they are framing problems and concerns. This goal is to understand where attitude and aptitude intersect for this novice, at this time.

Until you know the new teacher's perspective, or what resources, or concerns the novice comes with, you can't know which stance to take. The answers to clarifying questions help the mentor to determine the direction of the conversation and what might be a productive shift in stance (See Table 3.3: The Continuum of Interaction).

Table 3.3 The Continuum of Interaction

Mentor / Information, Analysis, Goals	Calibrating	Consulting	Collaborating (Beginning Teacher / Information, Analysis, Goals)	Coaching
Guiding question	Given teaching and learning standards and present performance, what do the data indicate as growth areas for this teacher?	What information, ideas, and technical resources might be the most useful for me to offer this teacher at this time?	What are some ways to balance my contributions with this teacher's knowledge and experience?	What inquiries might stimulate/stretch this teacher's thinking at this time?
Function	• Clarifying standards • Using data to highlight gaps/gains between expected standards and present results • Identifying problems/successes • Naming necessary outcomes	• Contextualizing standards • Using data to illustrate gaps and gains between standards and present results • Offering information, ideas, and technical resources	• Jointly contextualizing standards • Using data to collaboratively analyze gaps and gains between standards and present results • Co-generating information and ideas • Co-analyzing problems	• Referencing standards as a focal point for inquiries • Using data to inquire about gaps and gains between standards and present results • Stimulating teacher idea production • Supporting teacher problem framing • Inquiring to internalize habits of mind for effective planning, reflecting, and problem solving
Role in planning for action	• Focusing teacher actions/goals • Defining success criteria • Establishing timelines	• Proposing teacher action/goals • Clarifying success criteria • Recommending timelines • Providing problem analysis	• Co-constructing teacher actions/goals • Co-developing success criteria • Agreeing on timelines	• Exploring teacher actions/goals • Eliciting success criteria • Clarifying timelines
Cues	• Credible voice • Using neutral language, as in *"The student's work. . ." "This example. . ." "This standard. . ."*	• Credible voice • Using neutral language or personal pronouns, as in *"I think that. . ." "It is important to. . ." "Here is one way to think about that"*	• Approachable voice • Collective pronouns, as in *"Let's think about. . ." "How might we. . ."*	• Approachable voice • Second person pronouns, as in *"What are some of your. . .?" "How might you. . .?"*
Cautions	• Take care not to let personal preferences become prescriptions. Judgments must be supported by clear, external criteria/standards. • Use literal observation notes, classroom artifacts and assessment data to avoid subjectivity or bias.	• Monitor and manage the impulse to help or rescue. Stay learning-focused and don't let personal passion overcome patience with the developmental process. • Be aware that overuse of the consulting stance may build dependency on the mentor for problem solving.	• Resist the impulse to dominate the conversation and provide the bulk of the analysis and thinking. • Monitor for balance in idea production. Don't allow personal enthusiasm or preferences to override the intention to co-create ideas and options.	• Reduce potential frustration by posing developmentally appropriate questions. Questions should stretch, not strain thinking. • Be sure to construct inquiries that allow for multiple responses and do not signal that there is a preferred answer.

Typically, the conversation opens somewhere between collaborating and coaching. For example, the mentor might inquire or invite co-construction of information (See Table 3.4: Starting the Conversation).

Once an issue has been named and framed, mentors choose the most appropriate stance for approaching the situation. This choice depends upon the knowledge, skills, and emotional resources that the beginning teacher brings to the situation. The choice also depends on the knowledge, skills, and emotional resources of the mentor. Novice mentors often leap to telling or advising because of a sense of urgency or because they lack repertoire within the consulting stance, skipping over the problem framing and the naming of principles of practice, moving directly to "Here is what you need to do", or "Here's how I do it." They also often lack repertoire for operating within the coaching or collaborating stances, or have discomfort with the calibrating stance (See Table 3.5: Mentor Moves When Navigating the Continuum of Interaction).

Table 3.4 Starting the Conversation

Mentor Move	What is it?	Might look/sound like
Respond to novice concern with a paraphrase and inquire	Acknowledging the novice's perspective with the paraphrase establishes readiness for thinking that provides emotional support balanced with cognitive challenge.	*"So you're finding that some of your ELL's are struggling to keep up and you want to find methods to keep everyone engaged and challenged. What are some critical times when this issue occurs?"*
Refer to ongoing goal(s) and inquire	Facilitating the novice's professional vision and reinforcing continuous learning by keeping the conversation goal focused.	*"Given your professional goal for offering clear and efficient directions, what are some things you're noticing about your progress?"*
Present data and inquire/ or invite collaborative conversation	Reinforcing teaching and learning standards and building the capacity to use formative and summative data for self-assessment.	*"As you compare these writing samples to the performance criteria, what are some growth areas you're noticing?"* or *"Let's compare these writing samples to the performance criteria and identify some growth areas."*

> *"The mentor's role is to continually increase capacity and decrease dependency, thereby empowering and not enabling."*

Table 3.5   Mentor Moves When Navigating the Continuum of Interaction

Mentor Move	What is it?	Might look/sound like
Start the conversation in a coaching stance	An initial inquiry to get a sense of the novice's present perspectives, perceptions, and emotions.	Opening with choice: *"There are several options for our time today, where would you like to start?"* Build on experience: *"Given the behavioral interventions you've been trying out, what are some changes you're noticing?"* Acknowledging the moment: *"What are some things that happened today that were really satisfying/concerning?"*
End the conversation in a coaching stance	A final inquiry checks for the new teacher's understanding, agreement on goals, and clarity about next steps.	Generalizations: *"Given this conversation, what are some big ideas for you?"* Applications: *"Based on some of the ideas you've generated, what are your specific next steps?"*
Embrace the blurry boundaries of the collaborating stance	The collaborating stance scaffolds and stretches. It signals we're in this together and I assume your full input. Whether it's closer to the consulting or coaching end of the continuum, this stance has the widest range of application. At the consulting edge, the mentor offers information as a stimulus for co-construction. At the coaching edge, the mentor invites co-construction with an open-ended question.	*"Given the importance of getting student attention before giving directions, let's generate some focusing strategies that might work in your classroom."* or *"Let's generate some attention moves that might work in your classroom. What's one that comes to mind?"*
Use the consulting stance as a resource for stimulating thinking, not fixing the problem	Providing information, e.g., technical support, data analysis, instructional strategies, and problem frames to support thinking in the moment and, more importantly, for transfer to future practice over time.	*"You need to be explicit and intentional to create a thoughtful classroom. Several options for encouraging student thinking include: increasing your wait time and letting kids know why; using a think-pair-share pattern; and using open-ended syntax in your questions."* *"You've been describing this student's behavior as disrespectful. It's possible that he uses language that he hears from others, and right now is the only way he knows how to express himself."*
Apply the calibrating stance to judge the performance, not the person	Teaching and learning standards are the drivers of learning-focused conversations. Literal, objective data are the focal point for productive interactions. In the calibrating stance mentors identify gaps and gains. They offer feedback on performance, not on the beginning teacher's attitudes and aptitudes.	*"These data indicate that 63% of the students are proficient in this math standard at this point. It is essential that students master this concept to support the necessary understanding for units that follow."* *"More and different students participated in this lesson than in the previous lesson I observed. This increase reflects real growth both in communicating with students and establishing a positive learning environment."*

Focusing the Conversation: Establishing the Third Point

Skilled mentors create a clear focus by establishing a third point for the conversation. The third point is a way to display and place attention on visual information. As contrasted with two-point communication, which is eye-to-eye and relationally focused, three-point communication shifts the cognitive and emotional energy away from the mentor/novice relationship, placing the attention on an item or artifact. Effectively applying a third point includes non-verbal elements and verbal elements. Non-verbal elements include a physical shift from face-to-face to eyes on the data and a physical reference to the data source with a still hand, or frozen gesture. Verbal elements include using a credible voice and neutral pronouns when referring to data or information.

The third point is an observable focusing agent. In most cases, teaching or learning standards and performance rubrics are necessary third points for productive learning-focused conversations. Other relevant examples might include a work product, such as a lesson plan, samples of student work, or observational data. It can involve a demonstration or the observation of an event, such as a model lesson, a video, or a specific student's behavior.

Physically referencing the third point in a space off to the side between the parties provides a psychologically safe place for information, concerns, and problems. This subtle use of space and gesture depersonalizes ideas. It is now not the mentor's information or problem, the colleague's information or problem, nor even our information or problem. It is simply information or a problem about which and with which to think. Information placed as a third point frees the colleague to accept, modify or reject the idea as an idea. Without this subtle, but critical distancing, a new teacher might feel trapped in a web of relationship, and have difficulty freely accepting or rejecting an idea, for fear of hurt feelings. Thus, placement of the conversational focus creates a triangle, either literally or referentially, keeping the conversational container psychologically safe (See Figure 3.3: Three-Point Communication).

Mentors can employ a third point from any stance. The Calibrating and Consulting stances are predominantly three-point interactions. When shifting to the Collaborating or Coaching stances, there is a greater amount of pivot between three and two-point communication.

WHEN USING A THIRD POINT

- Sit with dominant hand towards the colleague at 90° angle
- Eyes on the data/ information
- Frozen gesture
- Neutral pronouns

NEUTRAL PRONOUNS

- These students seem to. . .
- The performance scores indicate. . .
- The writing samples demonstrate. . .
- This script of student responses shows. . .

Applying the Third Point

Communications expert Michael Grinder (2006) describes the influence of three-point communication. To maximize the effectiveness of the third point, purposeful attention must be placed on the physical elements. The mentor and beginning teacher sit at a 90° angle so the mentor can pivot from two-point to three-point communication. The mentor's dominant side is toward the beginning teacher so that shifting to the third point closes the mentor's body, directing attention towards the object. This relational exit assigns any emotions to the object, not the relationship.

SOME EXAMPLES OF THIRD POINTS

- Teaching/learning standards
- Samples of student work
- Rubrics
- Lesson plans
- Curriculum guides
- Formative and summative assessments
- Individualized Education Plan(s)
- New teacher portfolios
- Videos
- Parent letters, communications

Figure 3.3 Three-Point Communication

Imagine, for instance, a mentor and a fourth-grade teacher are meeting to discuss expository writing. They are reviewing students' writing samples. The mentor enters the conversation in a Coaching stance, focusing on one student's work. The students' writing samples and the writing standards function as third points.

Mentor: *"What are some things you're noticing about this student's work as it compares to the writing standards?"*

New Teacher: *"Well, I think the writing has improved, but I'm not really sure about which parts meet the standards."*

At this point, the mentor might shift to a Calibrating stance, sharing what she notices about the work and making specific references to the writing standards, pointing out examples in the work that meet or don't meet the expectations.

Mentor: *"So you can see growth, but not specifically which skills are improving. Comparing this sample with the standard for word choice, for example, this student is a three on the writing rubric because. . ."*

She might then use a similar pattern with another student sample. In this way, the novice has several concrete examples that clarify and calibrate the standards as well as a model of a more sophisticated lens for examining student writing. Continuing in the Calibrating stance, the mentor would widen the conversation to the whole class.

Mentor: *"In reviewing the whole class, it appears that 40% of the students are writing at this level. While it's an improvement since last month, it will be important to design targeted instruction so that every student meets the standard for word choice."*

Using a collection of instructional resources as the third point, the mentor now moves to a Consulting stance.

Mentor: *"At this stage, here are several strategies that would produce skill in both oral and written language."*

Pivoting to two-point communication in a Collaborative stance, the mentor might suggest shared idea generation and co-planning.

Mentor: *"Let's generate some pros and cons for each strategy and then brainstorm ideas for incorporating one or more of them into upcoming lessons."*

The conversation would end in a Coaching stance by clarifying next steps.

Mentor: *"Given your choices at this point, what are some next steps?"*

Awareness & Action: Applying the Third Point

Awareness:

1. How might three-point communication focus your conversations?

2. What are some topics where a third point might make it psychologically safer for your new teacher to engage?

3. What are some potential third points you might bring to your meetings?

Action:

1. Practice the shift from two-point to three-point communication in low threat situations.

2. Focus on intonation patterns, keeping your eyes on the data/information and using a frozen gesture.

Flexibility in Stance: Monitoring in the Moment

If the beginning teacher appears stumped and lacks repertoire for contributing ideas, the mentor then switches stances. As a consultant, the mentor might propose some ways to think about a problem or concern, offer options for action, and then flex to a coaching stance to help the new teacher consider and reflect upon the options and appropriate steps to take when clear choices emerge. By attending carefully to the new teacher's thinking and idea generation, a mentor can determine her actions and decide whether to remain in a coaching stance or flex to collaborating or back to consulting.

At other points, the mentor might be in a coaching or collaborating stance and it becomes clear that the novice is unable to generate ideas or options. The aware mentor then flexes to a consulting stance to offer information and perspectives. With this refined third point established, he or she can then slide back to collaborating or coaching, whichever is now most appropriate. This pattern of flexing across the continuum continues as needed throughout the conversation.

Differentiated Conversations

It is apparent that all new teachers are not alike. Customizing interactions for these differences is an important skill set for mentors. The mentor's role is to continually increase capacity and decrease dependency, thereby empowering and not enabling. Expertise navigating the Continuum of Interaction is a key resource for matching mentor moves to teacher needs.

The Intersection of Attitude and Aptitude

New teachers come with differing levels of independence, confidence, enthusiasm, awareness, knowledge, and skill. These attributes vary in intensity and intersect with one another resulting in differing degrees of receptivity to new learning, readiness to reflect, and resilience when confronting challenges.

We call these variables the intersection of attitude and aptitude (see Figure 3.4: The Intersection of Attitude and Aptitude). In the text below we offer mentor moves that differentiate for each quadrant.

Figure 3.4 The Intersection of Attitude and Aptitude

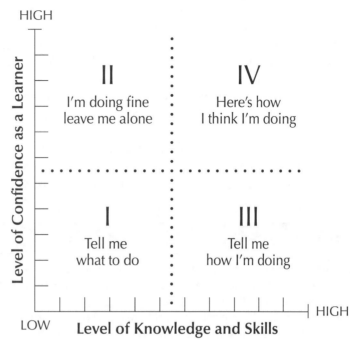

QUADRANT I: "TELL ME WHAT TO DO"

The new teacher in this quadrant lacks both confidence and skill. These teachers often appear overwhelmed, stumped when problem solving, and fearful of making a mistake. Instead of relying on their own decision making, they seek sure answers from their mentors. Rather than think for themselves, they want rescue and recipes. When working with Quadrant I teachers, the mentor's goal is to scaffold choice-making and experimentation for increasing confidence as a learner. In learning-focused conversations, there is likely to be a higher percentage of time in the consulting stance (See Table 3.6: Mentor Moves for Quadrant I Teachers).

Table 3.6 Mentor Moves for Quadrant I Teachers

Mentor Move	What is it?	Might look/sound like
Focus on consulting strategies such as: What, Why, How	Consulting provides information for the novice to process, thereby increasing repertoire and the confidence to apply it. For example, the What, Why, How strategy connects specific actions with the reason for choosing them. Making this explicit connection increases intentional choice-making, and the ability to generate additional purposeful strategies.	*"Always provide the expectations and criteria for success with the learning outcome/product for each lesson. This is important because the clearer students are about what constitutes good work, the more they can self-assess and self-regulate. You might do this by reviewing and posting a rubric related to a project or assignment."*
Emphasize the application of criteria for choice-making during the conversation	Consult and collaborate to generate criteria for choosing instructional strategies. Applying criteria to options exercises the ability to make effective choices with increased confidence.	*"So you're establishing group work with your 8th graders. Some criteria to draw upon for balanced groups might include academic performance, social skills, and diversity (gender, race, ethnicity). Let's generate an observation checklist to use when monitoring group work. One thing to look for is balanced participation. What else?"*

QUADRANT II: "I'M DOING FINE. LEAVE ME ALONE"

The new teacher in this quadrant has more confidence than skill. These teachers will often deflect the mentor's overtures, claiming all is well. These teachers often appear highly certain, and use the language of current initiatives and buzzwords, but without exhibiting the related teaching behaviors. Instead of seeking feedback and counsel from their mentor, they assume they're going in the right direction. Rather than reflect on their own practices, they close their door and stumble forward. When working with Quadrant II teachers, the mentor's goal is to increase awareness, provide tools for monitoring effectiveness, and motivate objective self-assessment. Therefore, in learning-focused conversations, there is likely to be a higher percentage of time in the calibrating stance (See Table 3.7: Mentor Moves for Quadrant II Teachers).

Table 3.7 Mentor Moves for Quadrant II Teachers

Mentor Move	What is it?	Might look/sound like
Increase awareness by using low-inference, literal data and teaching/learning standards as a third point to calibrate present practice to expectations.	Standards and evidence offered non-judgmentally provide a foundation for learning. Using three-point communication takes the spotlight off the teacher, puts the attention on the data and makes it safe to explore.	*A mentor might focus on observational data about the beginning teacher's use of questioning and wait time and make connections with the related standard at the highest end of performance. Highlight success "this is significant because. . ."*
Inquire for details and specific examples; and offer them if the novice is unable to do so.	Asking first is always respectful and presumes capacity. Specific details frame the conversation concretely. These key examples open the territory for data-based analysis and planning.	*"Given the value of high levels of student engagement, what are some examples of recent lesson designs where you built this into your planning?"*

QUADRANT III: "TELL ME HOW I'M DOING"

The new teacher in this quadrant is competent, but not confident. They have fundamentally sound knowledge and skills but are insecure about their effectiveness. These teachers seek external validation and rely on the mentor's judgment, instead of relying on their own. Rather than trying new ideas to expand their repertoire, they stay in their comfort zone by sticking with what has been working. When working with Quadrant III teachers, the mentor's goal is to provide tools for monitoring practices, support internalization of criteria for success, and encourage self-assessment. In learning-focused conversations, the mentor is likely to operate more of the time in the collaborating stance to balance emotional support with cognitive challenge (See Table 3.8: Mentor Moves for Quadrant III Teachers).

Table 3.8 Mentor Moves for Quadrant III Teachers

Mentor Move	What is it?	Might look/sound like
Collaboratively generate success criteria and self-monitoring tools	The coaching edge of the collaborative stance balances supports with challenges and pushes thinking but does not overwhelm. Creating success criteria fuels professional vision and supports the idea that the locus of control lives within the teacher.	*"Let's generate some criteria your students might use to assess the effectiveness of their collaborative groups."*
Extrapolate principles of practice from reflecting on success and generate additional strategies that exemplify that principle	The consulting edge of the collaborative stance balances cognitive challenge with support to increase awareness of patterns of success and generalize principles of practice to transfer to future lessons.	*"So, we're naming some big ideas here. They are that when students develop success criteria for their projects they increase collective commitment to project success and more readily initiate course corrections as they work together. Based on those understandings, let's generate some ways to apply those principles to your next round of projects."*

QUADRANT IV: "HERE'S HOW I THINK I'M DOING"

The new teacher in this quadrant has a strong internal locus of control. They recognize that their choices and actions are what produce results. These teachers have the confidence to try new things and are willing to learn from mistakes. They are reflective and self-disclosing about progress. They use data to set and pursue new goals and understand that teaching is continuous learning. When working with Quadrant IV teachers, the mentor's goal is to help internalize the voice of expertise. They expand the new teacher's lenses for observing the results of their practice, accessing their options, and making increasingly effective choices. In learning-focused conversations, a high percentage of the time will be in the coaching stance (See Table 3.9: Mentor Moves for Quadrant IV Teachers).

Table 3.9 Mentor Moves for Quadrant IV Teachers

Mentor Move	What is it?	Might look/sound like
Ask questions that require thought, not description	Description questions consume limited time and do not add value to the conversation. Questions that explore for purposes, criteria, and data sources for choices or actions stimulate thought.	*"What are some of the data you collect to assess the effectiveness of your lab groups?"* *"What are some of the purposes for having your students share science stories they find in the news and online?"*
Use teaching standards as a third point to widen the lenses for examining practice and setting new goals	Standards provide a fine-grained look at the complexities of teaching. Using the exemplars within and across standards allows the focus to go deeper, within a given standard or wider to include connections to related standards.	*"Based on the standards establishing a positive climate for learning, what are some of the things you're learning about giving students feedback about their behavior?"*

Versatility Matters

Expert mentoring requires a repertoire of knowledge and skills for engaging new teachers in productive formal and informal conversations. These professional resources provide the foundation for operating along the Continuum as we interact with colleagues. Having access to one's repertoire opens up possibilities for successful mentoring interactions and offers options for consideration when a given approach is not working. Knowing what we know and don't know helps us to identify gaps in our repertoire so we can consciously expand our own capacities as growth agents.

Versatility matters. In any given conversation, any one of the four stances may be appropriate. By reading the verbal and nonverbal cues of the colleague with whom we are engaged and responding accordingly, we can then flex along the Continuum to support learning and growth. This flexibility in stance is the key to successful mentoring relationships. If our goal is to increase our new teachers' capacities for self-direction, we need to continually offer opportunities to think, reflect, and problem solve within the flow of the real work of learning to teach. Our ability to continually anticipate, monitor, and flex our stance across the Continuum of Interaction is a vital component in developing and maintaining learning-focused relationships.

Awareness & Action: Differentiating Conversations

Awareness:

Think about where your beginning teacher might fit on the Attitude/Aptitude scale.

1. What are some mentor moves that might be effective?

Action:

1. Assess your present use of the consulting moves.
2. Choose several consulting moves that might be useful additions to your repertoire.
3. Assess your present use of the collaborating moves.
4. Choose several collaborating moves that might be useful additions to your repertoire.

SECTION 4 | Learning-Focused Verbal Tools

RELATIONSHIP and learning are intertwined both in-the-moment and over time. Learning and thinking draw upon person-to-person and person-to-idea connections. These linkages require purposeful assembly. Subtle moves and behaviors nurture the mentoring relationship and desired thinking processes. Our consciousness of these components helps us to support productive outcomes. Inattention to these elements can hinder or block interpersonal and intellectual connection-making.

Applying Verbal Tools

Language and thinking are interactive processes. Each energizes the other. Each limits the other. Learning-focused conversations create, nourish, and sustain language development. The ultimate goal of such conversations is to support language and thinking production capacities in our beginning teachers. In the process, we often extend our own thinking and language production capacities.

How we interact with others matters as much as the content about which we interact. Thoughtful, thought-filled conversations require carefully constructed containers to support them. We craft these containers from several important verbal elements drawn from a learning-focused toolkit (See Figure 4.1: Learning-focused Toolkit).

Figure 4.1 Learning-Focused Toolkit

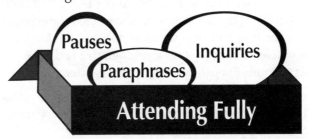

The learning-focused toolkit presented in this chapter adds verbal elements to the physical foundation of attending fully described in Section 2. These tools include pauses, paraphrases, and inquiries. They are essential resources for guiding planning, reflecting, and problem solving conversations (See Section 2) and operate in concert with the Continuum of Learning-focused Interaction (See Section 3).

Providing Emotional Safety

Current research in neurobiology stresses the primacy of emotional processing and its direct links to higher cognitive processes. There are a greater number of neural fibers running from the brain's emotional centers up into logical/rational areas than there are running in the opposite direction.

> "The limits of my language mean the limits of my world."
> - Gloria Steinem

Threat or perceived threat inhibits thinking. Our brains are wired to detect the subtleties of muscle tension, posture, gesture, and vocal stresses that signal danger in any form. Incoming sensory data moves through biochemically driven switching centers in the limbic portion of the brain. Branching circuits direct the signals first to a structure called the amygdala, which scans, codes, and assesses the present experience for signs of danger. If the incoming information passes this test, another circuit fires and sends the message to the prefrontal lobes of the cortex for processing. If the amygdala detects any threat, it either inhibits or aborts this upshifting. A classic example of this phenomena is watching a student panic and freeze when asked a question in class. The answer may be in his brain but it is not biochemically accessible in that instance. We must provide emotional safety to produce cognitive complexity.

Purposeful Pausing

The pace of a conversation affects both the emotional and intellectual climate. Frequent, well-placed pauses contribute to a beginning teacher's confidence and capacity. For most people, consciously pausing to provide a space for thinking requires patience and practice. Silence can feel uncomfortable. Mentors often perceive the lack of an immediate response as a struggle and rescue their beginning teacher with advice and suggestions. The fast pace of our world tends to support the belief that there is a relationship between speed and intelligence. Complex thinking takes and requires time.

The mentor's intent in learning-focused interactions is to provide thoughtful paraphrases and questions that invite a beginning teacher to think deeply and diversely. Patiently providing quiet time for uninterrupted thinking supports this intention and can be one of our greatest gifts to the novice.

Science educator and researcher Mary Budd Rowe (1986) first noticed the positive effects of pausing in the classroom. She labeled these pauses wait time. Wait time is the length of time we pause to allow thinking. Rowe suggested three to five seconds. Higher level cognitive tasks may require a full five seconds or more. English language learners often require twice that.

In learning-focused conversations there are four influential opportunities for pausing: after inquiring, after the teacher responds, before a paraphrase, and after a paraphrase.

Four Types of Pauses

PAUSE AFTER ASKING A QUESTION:
This pause allows time for thinking and signals your belief in your colleague's capacity and willingness to think. A minimum of three seconds is recommended; higher level cognitive tasks may require five seconds or more.

PAUSE AFTER TEACHER'S RESPONSE:
This is the pause provided after the teacher's initial response, allowing the colleague to mentally retrieve additional and/or related information. For many people, thinking comes in bursts. This pause stimulates deeper thinking and often results in elaboration or extension of the initial idea.

PAUSE TO ENHANCE THINKING & THOUGHTFULNESS

- PAUSE after asking a question
- PAUSE after a colleague responds
- PAUSE before paraphrasing
- PAUSE after paraphrasing

Pause Video
vimeo.com/miravia/pause

PAUSE BEFORE PARAPHRASING:

This pause is the length of time the mentor takes before responding. This type of pause provides the necessary space to thoughtfully construct language, models the importance of thinking before responding, and displays value for thoughtfulness.

PAUSE AFTER A PARAPHRASE:

This pause provides time for beginning teachers to reflect on how the paraphrase organizes or expresses their thinking. It supports confirmation or correction of the paraphrase, ensuring the mentor's understanding. In addition, this pause provides the mentor with time to consider options: craft an inquiry or shift stance on the Continuum of Interaction.

Making Pause a Habit

Our use of pause emerges from cultural and personal experience. This history is the source of comfort or discomfort with silence in conversations. While it is counterintuitive in Western culture, slowing down actually improves the efficiency of our interactions because it reduces threat and increases clarity.

Pausing is a foundational skill in learning-focused conversations because it supports focus on the other person and reinforces the intention to encourage thoughtfulness. Often our responses are unconscious. Being aware of pausing and creating new habits is an important goal for mentors.

When a mentor meets with her new teacher, time pressure and a sense of responsibility for success influence the pacing of the conversation and may inhibit taking time for pausing. Once the mentor becomes aware of this limiting communication pattern, opportunities open for establishing new routines. When the mentor is aware of the value of silence, the new routine is a purposeful pause and the new reward is appreciating the increasing the capacity and confidence of the beginning teacher to think. (See Figure 4.2: The Habit Cycle/Breaking the Habit Cycle).

Figure 4.2 The Habit Cycle/Breaking the Habit Cycle

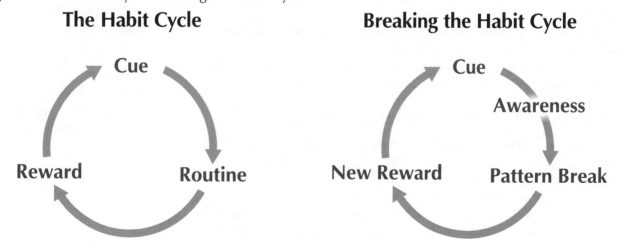

The mentor asks a question and the beginning teacher is silent (cue). This quiet creates discomfort for the mentor, who provides the answer to the question (routine). This response pattern alleviates the discomfort of silence and fills the void with information (reward).

Awareness & Action: The Power of Pausing

Awareness:

1. What are some of your own pausing tendencies?

2. What cues might trigger discomfort with pausing?

Action:

1. In low threat settings, such as a social occasion or a casual conversation, make an effort to be conscious about pausing.

2. Monitor your own use and start with the pause you use the least. Purposefully develop a new pattern by intentionally lengthening your pause. Try counting silently to four or increase your acuity by attending to non-verbal signs that your partner is thinking. Notice the results for others and for you as a growth agent.

Entering the New Teacher's World: Using Paraphrase

The purposeful use of paraphrase signals our full attention. It communicates that we understand the beginning teacher's thoughts, concerns, questions, and ideas, or that it is important to us to do so. By signaling that we are listening, we earn relational permission to inquire for details and press for elaboration. Without the paraphrase, such inquiries may feel like interrogations and suggestions may seem like impositions. Well-crafted paraphrases align the speaker and responder, establishing understanding and communicating regard. Questions, no matter how well-intended, distance by degrees the asker from the asked.

Well-crafted paraphrases with appropriate pauses trigger more thoughtful responses than questions alone. Skillful paraphrasing is a process, driven by the intention to support thinking and problem solving and the attention of the paraphraser, who listens fully for the essence of the message.

Skilled paraphrasing treats responses as gifts. In addition to their invitational qualities, effective paraphrases contain three important elements: they label the speaker's content, they often label the speaker's emotions about the content, and they structure the content for deeper exploration. The paraphrase reflects a speaker's thinking back to the speaker for further consideration. It connects the speaker and the listener in a flow of discourse.

Four Types of Paraphrase, Four Intentions

Versatility in use of paraphrase gives a mentor an effective repertoire for supporting growth and enhancing relationship. Four types of paraphrases, with four different intentions, widen the range of possible responses for learning-focused mentors. The four types, or paraphrase categories, are Acknowledge and Clarify, Summarize and Organize, Shift Level of Abstraction Up, and Shift Level of Abstraction Down. While each supports relationship and thinking, there is no formula for which type to use in any given instance. Cues from the speaker will help suggest an appropriate response. Versatility in use of paraphrase gives a skillful mentor a wider range of effective response options.

FOUR DO'S OF PARAPHRASE

· Avoid personal pronouns: "It seems to me. . .", "What I hear you saying. . ."

· Less is more: Keep the response shorter than the initiating statement

· Wait until the speaker is finished: Listen without interruption before paraphrasing

· Use tone to communicate intention: Invite confirmation or correction using an approachable voice

Acknowledge and Clarify
Paraphrase Video
vimeo.com/miravia/acknowledge

Summarize and Organize
Paraphrase Video
vimeo.com/miravia/summarize

ACKNOWLEDGE AND CLARIFY

By restating the essence of someone's statements, acknowledge and clarify paraphrases provide an opportunity to identify and reflect content and emotions. By design, they communicate our desire to understand, and our value for the person and what he or she is feeling and saying. Notice the intentional elimination of the personal pronoun I in the paraphrase video examples.

SUMMARIZE AND ORGANIZE

Summarize and organize paraphrases offer themes and containers which shape the initiating statement or separate jumbled issues. This type of paraphrase is useful when there's been a great deal said in a long stream of language, or when there is a complex issue with many parts or details. This type of paraphrase captures the key elements and offers some organization to which the speaker can react. It offers a structure to the initiating statement. These organizing options include: containers or categories, compare/contrast, large themes, or a sequence or hierarchy.

SHIFT LEVEL OF ABSTRACTION

A paraphrase that shifts the level of abstraction is a response that moves language, and therefore, thinking to a higher or lower conceptual level. The intention of this paraphrase is to illuminate large ideas or categories, often leading the speaker to new discoveries, exploring potentially broad applications or determining possibilities for transfer. Or, when shifting down, this paraphrase focuses and clarifies, increasing precision of thinking and understanding for both parties.

SHIFT LEVEL OF ABSTRACTION UP

This form of paraphrase moves language to higher conceptual levels by naming the big ideas including concepts, values, beliefs, assumptions, and goals. This shift up is a way of helping new teachers explore a bigger picture and provides a wider context for their thoughts. Mentors choose this paraphrase when a new teacher offers lots of details or seems to have a narrow perspective on the topic being described.

A SCAFFOLD FOR CRAFTING PARAPHRASES

ACKNOWLEDGE AND CLARIFY

- So, you're feeling ____
- You're noticing that __
- In other words _____
- You're suggesting that __

SUMMARIZE AND ORGANIZE

- So, there seem to be two key issues here _____ and_____
- On the one hand, there is ___ and on the other hand, there is __
- For you then, several themes are emerging; _____
- It seems you're considering a sequence or hierarchy here; ___

SHIFT LEVEL OF ABSTRACTION (UP)

- So, a(n) _____ for you might be ____
  - concept
  - assumption
  - value/belief
  - goal
  - intention

SHIFT LEVEL OF ABSTRACTION (DOWN)

- So, a(n) _____ or you might be_____
  - example
  - non-example

This form of paraphrase is an essential resource for promoting transfer by providing a higher conceptual level to a specific action. For example, a mentor might paraphrase a teacher's description of students checking each other's writing for correct punctuation as peer review and then asking about other opportunities for student collaboration.

This is also the paraphrase mentors would apply to a problem solving conversation to expand the options for solution. For example, a mentor might paraphrase a teacher's concern about the math textbook being too difficult for his students as "you're looking for instructional materials to serve a variety learning needs", and then explore that broader idea.

SHIFT LEVEL OF ABSTRACTION DOWN

This form of paraphrase shifts the language to a lower conceptual level by offering examples or non-examples of the broader topic being described. This shift down is a way of grounding the thinking in specific instances and details to clarify and focus a beginning teacher's thinking. Mentors choose this paraphrase when a new teacher is thinking too globally and ideas need more precision.

Shift Level of Abstraction UP
Paraphrase Video
vimeo.com/miravia/shiftup

Shift Level of Abstraction
DOWN Paraphrase Video
vimeo.com/miravia/shiftdown

The Ladder of Abstraction

Language is a system of agreed upon labels. These labels reside at levels of abstraction ranging from more concrete or specific to more broad or generalizable. Each label represents a category. In his seminal work, linguist S.I. Hayakawa (1964) organizes language into levels of abstraction. He uses the metaphor of a ladder to illustrate these levels. The higher the rung of the ladder, the more subsets can be contained within the label. For example, the labels teacher and faculty member are at the same level of abstraction. Going up the ladder, one might find ascending rungs for staff member, educator, professional, public employee. Going down the ladder, descending rungs might include, history teacher, world history teacher, beginning world history teacher, and at the most concrete level, Ms. Santiago.

LADDER OF ABSTRACTION

Classroom Environment

Procedures & Routines

Managing Transitions

Activity Timer

Non-Verbal Cues When Paraphrasing

Individual's nonverbal communication patterns are as rich and as distinctive as is their spoken language. The brain and the body are an integrated system. What is happening on the inside is reflected in sometimes subtle, and in other times, overt ways by various parts of the body. Gestures accompany up to 90% of spoken language (McNeill, 2005). People talking on the phone gesticulate as they interact with others who cannot see them. Blind people gesture with the same frequency as do the sighted. These gestures enhance memory and comprehension skills and save energy by communicating essential information with minimal explanation. When a speaker says: "It's over there" while pointing to her right, the listener knows exactly where to locate the object in question without the need for further inquiry.

Gestures contribute to knowledge change by reducing the cognitive load on the speaker. Hand and arm movement efficiently convey concepts and ideas without the struggle to form language. This is especially important when the

> "Language is not an innocent reflection of how we think. The terms we use control our perceptions, shape our understandings, and lead us to particular proposals for improvement. We can see only as far as our language allows us to see."
>
> - Martin Haberman

PHYSICAL REFERENCING

· Characters in space

· Concepts in space

· Sequence or hierarchy

· Time orientation

Physical Referencing Video
vimeo.com/miravia/referencing

problem solver's brain is juggling fragments of thoughts and fragile connections that are just beginning to jell. Gestures are holistic so they communicate more than one piece of information at a time. For example, a speaker might indicate a specific person and the closeness of the relationship by hand position or motion that marks the space between them. The speaker may also physically reference where this person is above or below them in any hierarchy or organizational structure.

Gestures allow speakers to reveal novel ideas that may not totally align with current beliefs and conceptual frameworks. Such gestures may convey information or ideas that are outside of conscious awareness, revealing ideas that are not yet fully formed. These movements appear to slip past our self-monitoring systems. Emerging understandings are often given physical form before we can craft language to articulate them. For example, a speaker while describing her current workload simultaneously rotates her hands in a spiraling pattern that accelerates as she talks about the projects. The visual information might indicate an ever-increasing pace that is not yet given voice in her language.

Attention to these non-verbal messages increases the effectiveness and efficiency of our communication. The subtle cue, given and perceived, maximizes the clarity of the information and leads to greater productivity for both parties. By attending to the vocal patterns, such as rhythm, pitch, and pace that indicate changes in thinking or feeling, we gain rich information and insight into the thinking patterns of the other person. Intonation, emphasis, and volume are cues to what might be important or of primary concern in the narrative. Similarly, lengthy pauses, sighs, and repetition are also meaningful signals to note, and potentially respond to.

Marker Language	Marker Gestures
Verbal Stress	Physical Stress
• Volume	• Volume
• Emphasis	• Emphasis
Repetition	Repetition
Pace	Pace
Referencing	Referencing

Physical Referencing

As speakers employ marker words and marker gestures, they place characters in space. To interpret meaning and respond appropriately and strategically, note how near, on which side, and where the characters are in relation to one another. Concepts are located, and sometimes grouped or contrasted nonverbally, as well. Humans also gesture for time orientations, for example, a hand from back to front or left to right indicating past, present, and future. Gestural emphasis and patterns indicating a sequence or hierarchy of ideas or actions again give information about what might not be being said aloud, but what might matter to the speaker.

Individual's nonverbal communication patterns are as rich and as distinctive as is their spoken language. People have unique external cues to their internal thinking processes. While the patterns might be idiosyncratic, we can make some useful generalizations. For example, handedness plays a part in these patterns. Discerning hand dominance and observing marker cues is a useful communication tool. One study of politicians noted that right-handed candidates and office holders use their dominant hand to convey positive messages and their left to indicate negative messages. The pattern is reversed for left-handers (Casasanto & Jasmin, 2010).

Attention to these patterns becomes another form of deep listening. Paying attention to these spaces and/or patterns as part of the paraphrasing process increases the productivity of both attending to and responding to other people. By noting where in space a colleague places story elements and characters, we can paraphrase both verbally and nonverbally by referencing these locations with our own gestures and words.

Discerning and responding in kind to physical referencing is a subtle, but powerful skill that communicates understanding, increases psychological safety, and mediates thinking. By paying attention to these elements as they are communicated, and continuing to develop increased acuity, an observant communicator facilitates understanding and accelerates learning.

When Words and Gestures Don't Match

Gestures that are not congruent with speech are often an indication of a transitional stage between not knowing and knowing. The ground-breaking work of Susan Goldin-Meadow and her colleagues offers insight into our understanding of the role of gesture in the learning process (Goldin-Meadow & Wagner, 2005). For example, in one study, young children presented with a tall glass of water and the same volume in a low, wide dish will typically say that the taller vessel contains more water. They simultaneously point to show "this one's low and this one's high" to illustrate their claim. Children on the verge of understanding the concept of conservation will make the same verbal claim but accompany this with a two-handed gesture to indicate the width of the dish and a one-handed gesture to refer to the height of the taller container. Similar incongruencies between words and physical motions have been noted in 5-9-year-olds learning a balance task, 8-10-year-olds learning a math task, and adults learning a gears task.

Mentors can support learning and deeper understanding by noting these mismatches and responding to the learner through paraphrases, inquiries, and offering information. Goldin-Meadow links these transitional points to Vygotsky's zone of proximal development – the teachable moment (Goldin-Meadow, 2003; Vygotsky, 1978).

Awareness & Action: Practicing Paraphrase

Awareness:

1. Under what conditions do you choose to paraphrase (or choose not to paraphrase)?

2. How often do you paraphrase using formulaic language, such as "what I hear you saying" or "I think I hear you saying"?

3. What are some reactions or results you're aware of when you paraphrase?

Action:

1. Use the paraphrase scaffolds (p. 63) to support your construction of a paraphrase and eliminate the use of "I".

2. Set a goal of increasing your confidence and fluency with each type of paraphrase. Isolate the skill (e.g., focus on paraphrase in social or casual professional conversations) to make each type of paraphrase automatic.

3. Pay attention to your paraphrases and monitor for length. Be sure your paraphrase is shorter than the initiating statement.

Designing Questions to Promote Thinking

Skillful mentors are purposeful in their use of questions. Their inquiries communicate a spirit of curiosity and a desire to explore information and ideas. A mentor's linguistic repertoire includes language that broadens thinking, focuses thinking, and clarifies thinking. Learning-focused mentoring is a responsive process in which the mentor's inquiries interact with the beginning teacher's level of development and presenting concerns. Effective inquiries are open-ended, inviting multiple responses. A mentor's inquiries model and support expert thinking. Ultimately they transfer to become the novice's self-talk as they plan, reflect, and problem solve.

Questions that extend and illuminate thinking invite a wide range of potential responses. Language and thinking, once surfaced can always be honed and refined. But without it emerging, there is little with which to work. The intention of inquiry is to support a colleague in exploring issues, problems, concerns, and ideas.

Well-crafted inquiries integrate three essential elements: an invitation to engage, a cognitive process to stimulate thinking, and a topic to think about. These elements can be combined in a variety of ways and do not always appear in the same order (See Figure 4.3: A Template for Inquiry).

Figure 4.3 A Template for Inquiry

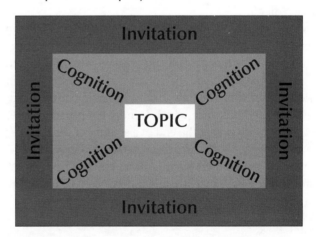

Invitational Inquiries

For beginning teachers, thinking aloud with their mentor involves both cognitive and relational risk. When we ask questions that push thinking beyond the recall level, there may be fear of judgment about the quality or completeness of the response. Adept mentors construct their questions to reduce this risk. Well-crafted questions produce high thought with low threat.

The important linguistic moves listed above and elaborated upon in the following pages need careful packaging to achieve their ultimate and most powerful impacts within mentoring conversations. This package is shaped by several critical paralinguistic and linguistic structures. The prefix para means above and around. In this case, the packaging elements are above and around the linguistic moves. These elements include such things as voice tone, inflection, and pace. In other words, how we say what we say. Also,

Template for Invitational
Inquiry Video
vimeo.com/miravia/inquiry

within the paraphrase and within inquiry, several language components influence the emotional and cognitive resources available in the moment to the beginning teacher.

We call this packaging the invitation. We are, in fact, creating the emotional environment that invites our colleague to think with us.

Elements of the Invitation: Creating the Conditions for Thinking

The invitation to think functions as a total package wrapped around our paraphrases and our inquiries. In Section 2: Structured Conversations: Maximizing Time and Attention, we explored patterns of attending fully. By attending fully, we signal that our complete attention is available for this conversation and that we intend no harm. To these tools we add two important layers: the tonal and the syntactical.

THE TONAL LAYER: APPROACHABLE VOICE

Listeners automatically assess the tone of the words they are hearing for any signs of threat. As described earlier, this rapidly firing safety assessment influences both what we hear and how we process the incoming information. For this reason, skillful mentors use a non-threatening intonation, or an approachable voice.

Approachable Voice

Michael Grinder, a classroom management expert and specialist in nonverbal patterns of communication (Grinder, 1997), labels the voice of invitation, an approachable voice. An approachable voice is well modulated and tends to rise at the end of the statement, paraphrase, or question, signaling openness and exploration encouraging the new teacher's participation. This intonation contrasts with the credible voice which is more evenly modulated with a flatter tone and tends to drop at the end of a statement. This voice pattern indicates that the speaker is sharing information and expertise. Voice choice signals the stance within which we are operating. The more approachable voice indicates a coaching stance; the more credible voice a calibrating or consulting stance.

SYNTACTICAL LAYER

Interpreting the syntactical structure of the message is the next filtering system in the human brain. Three key syntactical choices make it emotionally easier for the beginning teacher to think, and increase the options for thinking: plural forms, exploratory language, and non-dichotomous forms. These subtle elements can encourage or inhibit thinking and influence the quality of responses.

PLURAL FORMS

Plural forms indicate that there are multiple possible responses: goals instead of goal, concerns rather than concern. Spoken with an approachable intonation, plural forms suggest that all responses are acceptable and frees the novice from having to evaluate and sort at this point in the conversation.

EXPLORATORY LANGUAGE

Exploratory language has a tentative quality. Examples include words like some, might, seems, possible, and hunches. These terms, like the use of

SIX ELEMENTS OF THE INVITATION

· Attending Fully

· Approachable Voice

· Plural Forms

· Exploratory Language

· Positive Presupposition

· Non-dichotomous forms

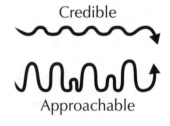
Credible

Approachable

SYNTACTICAL SUBSTITUTIONS

· the — some

· can/could — might

· is — seems

· why — what

Elements of the Invitation Video
vimeo.com/miravia/elements

**PATTERN OF
DISCOURSE**

listen/

pause/

paraphrase/

pause/

inquire

Credible Voice Video
vimeo.com/miravia/credible

Approachable Voice Video
vimeo.com/miravia/approachable

plurals, widen the potential range of response and reduce the need for surety. Words like can, could, and why tend to decrease the confidence of teachers who may interpret these words as questioning their capabilities for thought or indicate the need to justify their choices and actions. In addition, the words can/could may seem to seek premature commitment to ideas or actions, as in the question: "Given this issue, what could you do about it?" The use of why in an inquiry requires responders to explain or defend their thinking, as in the question "why did you choose that goal?"

Further, one unintended consequence of using why is that it can create a one up/one down dynamic, in that beginning teachers may feel forced to justify their ideas or reasoning.

NON-DICHOTOMOUS FORMS

Inquiries that are framed with open-ended, non-dichotomous forms add an additional element to the syntactical layer of the invitation. A non-dichotomous question is one which cannot be answered yes or no. For example, instead of asking "Did you notice any unusual behaviors?", ask "What are some of the behaviors you noticed?" In fact, by eliminating dichotomous stems such as "Can you," "Did you," "Will you," or "Have you," we invite thinking and communicate positive presupposition.

POSITIVE PRESUPPOSITIONS

Presuppositions are embedded in our language, not in the words, necessarily, but in the assumptions underlying the communication (Elgin, 2000). Human brains are wired to discern the embedded presuppositions in messages. All language expresses a mentor's presuppositions about the beginning teacher's professional capabilities. Negative presuppositions inhibit thinking while positive presuppositions stimulate it. Skilled mentors purposefully communicate belief in a colleague's capacity and willingness to engage by using positive presuppositions.

Consider these examples of invitational inquiries:

Instead of. . .	Try. . .
Can you think of a way to do that?	*How **might** you go about doing that?*
Why did you use those examples in your lesson?	*As you consider examples for use in your lessons, **what are some** criteria you use to make your choices?*
Have you considered using more technology in your lessons?	*Based on the power of technology to support learning, what **might** be **some** opportunities for using technology in your lessons?*
Do you have any ideas for ways to improve classroom management?	*Given the important connections between student learning and a well-managed classroom, **what are some** routines you might use with your class?*

Awareness & Action: Invitational Inquiry

Awareness:

1. What are some of your inquiry patterns? How much of the time are your inquiries invitational?

2. What are some things you notice about the effect of your inquiries on your beginning teacher's thinking?

Action:

1. In low threat settings, such as a social occasion or a casual conversation, monitor for dichotomous forms (yes/no questions such as can you/have you/did you?).

2. Choose and overlearn one or two invitational stems, such as What are some. . . and How might you. . . ? Use these inquiry starters with frequency in multiple settings.

3. When you prepare inquiries, in your own teaching or for print communication, edit your questions for invitational syntax and positive presuppositions.

Intention-Driven Questions: Providing Cognitive Focus

Planning, reflecting, and problem solving require specific ways of thinking. Learning-focused mentors craft inquiries that purposefully direct cognitive processes. For example, we develop expertise in planning by identifying, predicting, and sequencing. Similarly, teachers make sense of experience by inferring, comparing, and analyzing cause and effect. Productive reflection is a cluster of thinking processes: generalizing, hypothesizing, synthesizing, and applying. In problem solving conversations, the emphasis is on identifying and clarifying the problem, and cause and effect reasoning, seeking to determine underlying causes for the issue being explored. Inquiries that invite and focus thinking enhance professional capacity and self-directed learning. Each phase of the Conversation Templates is intended to focus and produce specific cognitive processes. The sidebar on this page offers a sampling of the cognitive processes related to each phase of the Conversation Templates.

Directing the Inquiry: The Topic

As described earlier, language ranges from higher to lower levels of abstraction. This essential concept applies to crafting productive inquiries. A skillful mentor's selection of topic is not a casual decision; purposefully naming the topic is a strategic choice. Mentors identify the topic based on the new teacher's developmental level, present capacities for managing cognitive challenge, and available data.

Higher levels of abstraction include the names of teaching domains, such as classroom instruction or learning environment. Lower levels of abstraction include success indicators, critical attributes or specific examples.

ACTIVATING

Recall, estimate, speculate, visualize, count, notice, list, describe, select, observe, predict, forecast

EXPLORING

Sort, relate, reason, explain, infer, contrast, compare, distinguish, analyze, weigh

INTEGRATING

Evaluate, classify, reflect, summarize, interpret, generalize, deduce, suppose, induce, postulate, hypothesize, theorize, conclude, prioritize

At a high level of abstraction, the mentor might ask: "What are some ways you monitor classroom management procedures?" At lower levels of abstraction, the mentor might inquire about instructional grouping, managing materials, furniture arrangements, or routines. To be even more concrete, the mentor might ask about size of groups, distribution of supplies, seating patterns, or attention moves.

"Well-crafted questions produce high thought with low threat."

Focusing the topic increases the time efficiency of the conversation by allowing the mentor to isolate critical areas while still inviting the beginning teacher's thinking about the topic. Further, a more directed question feels safer for the teacher because there is less ambiguity about potential appropriate responses.

Increasing the Impact of Inquiries: From Description to Thoughtfulness

Not all questions have equal value. Even when an inquiry contains all the element and includes an invitation, cognitive focus, and clear topic, it still might elicit description and not necessarily produce higher levels of thinking. When a mentor inquires for criteria for choice or success, source of data, evidence, or information and purposes or reasons, the beginning teacher needs to think deeply or more complexly (See Table 4.1: From Description to Thoughtfulness).

Table 4.1 From Description to Thoughtfulness

Beginning teacher says	Description question	Thoughtful inquiry
I want my students to be respectful of each other and I plan to do lots of collaborative work.	What are some collaborative projects you are considering?	Criteria: As you think about your outcome of respect, what criteria might you use to determine your initial projects? Or. . . to determine success?
I want my students to be respectful of each other and I plan to do lots of collaborative work.	What collaborative skills will your students need?	Source of data: Given that successful collaboration requires some fundamental skills, what are data sources you might use to determine student readiness?
I want my students to be respectful of each other and I plan to do lots of collaborative work.	What strategies will you use to develop collaborative skills?	Purpose: As you think about student collaboration, what are some things that are most important to you?

Inquiring to Clarify Thinking

Vague Language

Human communication is filled with vague language, statements with missing or overgeneralized information. Human language reflects these communication habits, offering surface vagueness that masks the rich details that lie beneath. For the sake of efficiency, our brain filters incoming and outgoing messages. One important way that mentors make a difference for novice teachers is by supporting precision in language, which in turn supports precision in thinking. By clarifying specifics, the attentive mentor can help shift a situation from one that might feel overwhelming to the novice, to one that is more emotionally and cognitively manageable. Like many mentoring skills, these inquiries are based on listening. In this case, it means listening for vague language and then deciding which terms, if clarified, would promote the most productive shifts in thinking.

Vague thinking and language patterns appear within five major categories: nouns and pronouns, verbs, comparators, rule words, and universal quantifiers (Bandler & Grinder, 1971). These categories guide the listening of the mentor. In many cases, more than one category of vagueness appears in the same statement. The attuned mentor selects a focus for clarification, paraphrases the essential ideas, then inquires for clarity within target areas. In all cases, mentors apply the pattern of pause, paraphrase, and inquire.

Vague Nouns and Pronouns

Vague nouns and pronouns occur commonly in everyday language. In schools we hear about, my students, the class, my fourth period, classroom management, student behavior, technology, the parents, the administration, central office and a host of other unspecified nouns. For many teachers, someone named they causes most of the problems in their class or school. We, us, and them are other possible sources of concern and/or joy.

If we hear a beginning teacher say, "my students don't understand fractions," we need to find out how many students are confused about fractions and what elements of fraction learning are most problematic to them. Without these essential details, we can't know where to target our energy and attention within the problem solving process. Narrowing the field of focus in this case might identify subsets of students with distinct learning needs that can be addressed systematically by the teacher and the students.

We would also need to determine the beginning teacher's definition of understand, which leads us to the next category of vagueness.

Vague Verbs

Planning, reflecting, and problem solving require specificity for focused action and personal learning. The term understand in the vignette above is a prime example. Once we have determined who has the problem, we need to clarify the goal of understanding. Just what does this teacher mean by understanding, and how will students display their understanding? With some novice teachers, these specifications may lead us to unpacking their understanding of fractions as well.

Teacher goal setting is a ripe area for probing the action words. Words like: plan, improve, design, modify, enhance, and prepare are all examples of unspecified verbs that have little meaning without clarification and details.

VAGUE LANGUAGE

· Nouns and Pronouns

· Verbs

· Comparators

· Rule Words

· Universal Quantifiers

Figure 4.4 Invitational Inquiry Exercise Mat

INVITATIONAL INQUIRY

Invitation

Cognition · Cognition · Invitation · Invitation · **TOPIC** · Invitation · Invitation · Cognition · Cognition · Invitation

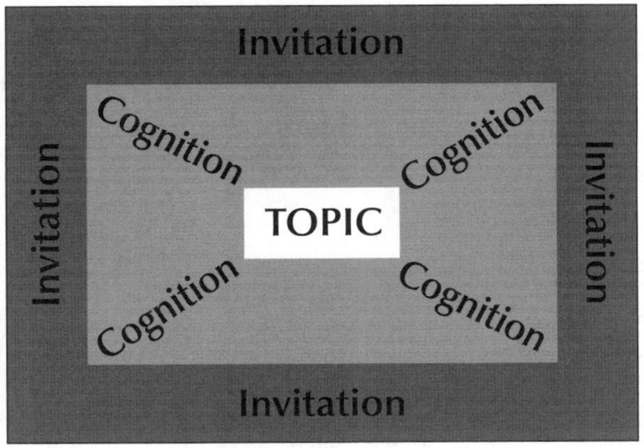

The Elements of the Invitation:

- Attending Fully
- Approachable Voice
- Plural Forms
- Exploratory Language
- Non-dichotomous Forms
- Positive Presuppositions

Syntactical Substitutions:

- the — some
- can/could — might
- is — seems
- why — what

Sample Stems:

- Given your knowledge of . . . .
- Based on your experience with . . . .
- Reflecting on . . . .
- As you consider . . . .

INVITATION	COGNITION	TOPIC
How might . . .	Predict	Outcomes
What would . . .	Recall	Curriculum
What are some . . .	Summarize	Instructional strategies
What might be some	Identify	Student readiness
In what ways . . .	Describe	Student behavior
How might you	Compare	Student work
What seem(s)	Contrast	Student engagement
Given your . . .	Prioritize	Performance standards
Based on . . .	Interpret	Assessment results
Reflecting on	Infer	Expectations
As you . . .	Conclude	Lesson
	Generalize	Materials
	Connect	Groups
	Apply	Classroom climate
	Evaluate	Procedures

EXAMPLES

What are some ways you are comparing this student's work to the performance standards?

(Invitation) (Cognition) (Topic) (Topic)

Recalling your concerns, how might you address this student's behavior?

(Cognition) (Invitation) (Topic)

As you consider these assessment results what seem to be priorities for next steps?

(Invitation) (Topic) (Invitation) (Cognition)

COMPARATORS

There are two primary types of vagueness relating to comparators; the criteria for comparison and the source of comparison. When our beginning teacher says, "Today's lesson was much better," two queries might be productive; "In what ways was it better?" and/or "What was it better than?" Until we discover the speaker's criteria for better, we don't know how to proceed with the conversation. Is this better a success to build on or are poorly understood factors at work here that leave this better a mystery? Other vague comparators are words like best, larger, slower, more, less, not, and least.

Mentors support novice teachers by helping them to specify their criteria and standards for comparison. This action supports rigor in planning and problem solving, which leads to targeted action and measurable signs of success. When a novice teacher says "I want students to get better results on my next quiz," the mentor would paraphrase and then inquire for the qualities that would define better results. For example, does the novice mean a higher class average or some other improvements in student responses?

We also often need to surface what's missing in the comparison. For example, was this lesson better than the best lesson the teacher has taught to date—or better than the worst? Our continued conversation would be quite different, depending upon the response.

RULE WORDS

We all have a set of rules that guide our ways of perceiving and operating in the world. We are not always conscious of these internal codes but they appear in our language when we say things like: I have to, I must, I can't, and I should have or I shouldn't have. When a mentor hears a beginning teacher use a phrase like those above, it may be appropriate to inquire for the rule behind the statement. "What are some conditions when that (rule) might or might mot apply?" or "What might happen if you didn't?" or "What are some factors that stop you from doing that?"

Intonation matters greatly here. The mentor's voice must be carefully modulated and nonthreatening to create a safe environment for exploring the internal rules governing the situation.

UNIVERSAL QUANTIFIERS

"All the parents of my class are upset about the new report card." "The students always get confused when I give directions." Linguists label words and phrases like: everyone, all, no one, never and always as universal quantifiers. They also use the term deity voice as a label for this type of language because these terms are spoken as if the statement possesses a universal truth of which everyone is aware. By clarifying the universal quantifier, a mentor helps her colleague ground the conversation with measurable details and supportable data. When the novice says, "Everyone in my class is struggling with this concept", the mentor would paraphrase and might respond: "As you think about your students, for what percentage of them is this the case?" "Has there ever been an instance when most of them were on time?"

Selecting Vague Terms for Clarification

Given the frequency of vague terms in our communications, it's important to recognize that not all vague terms need to be clarified. This is particularly true in learning-focused conversations. Mentors strategically choose the terms that might be the most productive avenues to determine the beginning teacher's meaning. Without shared understanding of the event, it is not possible for the mentor to know what to explore. For example, when a novice says, "My students are usually well-behaved", we don't know whether it's the entire class, what percentage of the time, or what her criteria are for good behavior. In the worst case, mentors assume understanding without clarifying and respond from their own way of thinking. In the example above, a mentor might impose her own definition of well-behaved, or assume that it's a large percentage of students, or that usually is more frequently than is true. There is potential for wasting valuable time if the conversation continues without clarification.

To develop the acuity for generating clarifying inquiries, mentors listen for, and inquire about: percentage, frequency, duration, criteria, descriptors, examples, and under what conditions (See Table 4.2: Clarifying Vague Language).

Table 4.3 Clarifying Vague Language

Listen/inquire for:	Beginning teacher might say:	Mentor move:
Percentage (how many?)	*"I can't seem to get my students to focus. We waste so much time just taking attendance and settling in each morning."*	*"Your students don't seem ready to tune in each morning. What percentage of your students display these behaviors?"*
Frequency (how often?)	*"I can't seem to get my students to focus. We waste so much time just taking attendance and settling in each morning."*	*"You're concerned about maximizing instructional time. How often does this problem occur?"*
Duration (how long?)	*"I can't seem to get my students to focus. We waste so much time just taking attendance and settling in each morning."*	*"So, you're losing instructional time each morning. How long does it typically take to get them settled?"*
Criteria (expectations?)	*"I can't seem to get my students to focus. We waste so much time just taking attendance and settling in each morning."*	*"You want your class to come to attention quickly each morning. What's your sense of how long that should take?"*
Descriptors (qualities?)	*"I can't seem to get my students to focus. We waste so much time just taking attendance and settling in each morning."*	*"You want students that know how to snap to attention. What might focus look and sound like?"*
Examples (which ones?)	*"I can't seem to get my students to focus. We waste so much time just taking attendance and settling in each morning."*	*"You're finding that time is consumed by non-instructional tasks. What are some examples of ways that students are wasting time?"*
Context (under what conditions?)	*"I can't seem to get my students to focus. We waste so much time just taking attendance and settling in each morning."*	*"You believe strongly that your students must transition into the classroom and quickly focus. Under what conditions might this expectation be less critical?"*

While each of these examples contain inquiries into vague language, some choices are likely to be more effective than others in producing clarity about the event or concern. For example, inquiring for how long it takes the students to settle is important information in aligning the mentor's understanding with the teacher's expectations. Or asking about the number of students who are inattentive would help determine the scope of the problem. Increased clarity makes planning, reflecting, and problem solving productive and growth promoting.

The Mentor's Toolkit

The learning-focused toolkit is a vital resource for communication between mentors and their beginning teachers. By applying these tools, growth oriented mentors offer support, create cognitive challenge, and facilitate professional vision for their developing colleagues. While the tools of pausing, paraphrasing, and inquiring operate in concert, each is easier to learn in isolation, with the goal of automated use in a variety of settings. Purposeful practice with each tool leads to fluent application within learning-focused conversations and fluid navigation of the Continuum of Interaction.

Awareness & Action: Clarifying Vague Language

Awareness:

1. What are some vague terms you use frequently in your own communication?

2. What are some vague terms you hear frequently from others (in person or in media)?

Action:

1. Spend fifteen minutes in a meeting or when listening to media to record vague terms you hear.

2. Review your beginning teacher's lesson plan. Identify vague language and consider how you might inquire for greater clarity.

SECTION 5 | Facilitating Professional Vision: From Novice to Expert Teaching

NO ONE is born knowing how to teach. Classroom instruction is one of the most complex intellectual and emotional tasks that any professional undertakes in our society; and the journey towards expertise is a lifetime's work. Successful journeys begin with skilled counsel and guidance.

In the opening of this book, we offer three goals for learning-focused relationships, suggesting that thoughtful mentors offer support, create cognitive challenge, and facilitate a professional vision for their beginning teachers. Each of these intentions requires a vision—of the growth potential of the new teacher, of the relationship between the mentor and a new colleague, and of the mentor's skill in sustaining productive learning for the novice.

According to psychologist Jean Piaget, learning is a process of disturbing current constructs with new experiences and exposure to novel ideas. Learners need to assimilate or accommodate these discoveries to form new conceptual understandings. Skillful mentors know when and how to gently disturb their new teacher's current state of development as they escort them on their journey from novice to expert teaching.

To focus this learning, mentors need frameworks and language for describing the intricacies of teaching. This complexity falls into two main areas: what professional teachers think about and pay attention to in their classrooms; and how they think about it before, during, and after instruction. This knowledge base organizes the expert teacher's planning, problem solving, and decision making. Mental access to these resources supports effective teaching practice that is goal-driven and targeted to the needs of individual students. These capabilities, brought to conscious attention, then guide the mentor's own teaching, modeling, and interactions with a new teacher.

There are no fast tracks to teaching expertise. The road is long, winding, and sometimes painful. Amid the noise and energy of schools and schooling, teaching can be a lonely profession. The early years for most novices are filled with doubts about personal effectiveness, teaching competence, and whether one has the personal learning capacities to master this complex profession.

Learning to teach means continually managing the disequilibrium that new questions and newly recognized quandaries produce. Given their limits of attention and their limits of craft knowledge, beginning teachers often do not know what they do not know. There is a vague awareness of some magic that the confident veteran next door seems to possess. But time and energy do not allow exploration of these seeming mysteries. Day-to-day survival and managing newly forming relationships with students, parents, and colleagues consumes most available time.

Mentoring, therefore, requires a continual balance of supporting current learning needs for the novice, with providing appropriate cognitive challenges for growth at opportune moments. It also means acknowledging the sense of loss and lowered confidence that often accompanies new awareness of knowledge and skill gaps. These are territories of constructive mismatch that require emotional sensitivity and scrupulous attention to the novice's emotional state and level of development. Clearly-defined teaching standards illuminate both the skill clusters and discrete skills that novices need to master on their journey towards increasing expertise. Mentors support this growth by helping beginning teachers develop clear mental representations— the what, why, and how of these standards. They then identity the mental and physical moves that their novices need to overlearn and automatize. Targeted and timely corrective feedback is the key to this skill development.

The information on the development of teaching expertise outlined in this section focuses the mentor's attention and frames this learning agenda. School-based curriculum initiatives intersect with this knowledge base to promote collegiality and learning communities in the school.

Deliberate Practice

All mental and physical skills are held as chunks in the brain. When these chunks are well integrated in our mental circuitry, we develop automaticity with a skill that is often outside of our awareness. This muscle memory supplies the ease of execution that we so admire in masters of any craft or art form. Successful coaches and mentors in all fields, from sports to music to medicine, help their learners break down the chunks in three levels: 1) They illuminate the big chunk or mega circuit that holds the task as a whole; 2) They break down the task into the smallest possible chunks that can be practiced as units; 3) They regulate performance time by slowing the action down for conscious skill development, then bringing it up to speed for skill execution. In this way, the coach helps the learner internalize the inner architecture of the desired skill or skill cluster (Coyle, 2009). For example, when teachers call a class to attention, they draw on physical skills for body placement in the teaching space, postural and tonal awareness to establish credibility, and verbal facility to convey the importance of their messages. Many novices struggle with this fundamental teaching task and waste valuable learning time trying to manage student energy and alertness.

The Nature of Expertise

One night at dinner with a good friend, who was a consultant to upscale restaurants, we had an insight. The establishment in which we were dining had a lovely ambiance, excellent food, and outstanding service. It was this latter attribute that prompted our friend to remark, "these servers have TRA; that's why the service is so good." TRA was his shorthand for Total Restaurant Awareness—the capacity to smoothly manage multiple tasks while paying attention to each element in the surrounding, including such factors as what is going on at each table, who needs more water, which party is ready for the check and how many of that night's specials are left in the kitchen. We realized that expert teachers have TCA, Total Classroom Awareness—the ability to attend to curriculum, lesson plans, content and performance standards, classroom management, and relationships with students while at the same time assessing current achievement levels and determining future learning needs within the lesson, the unit, the semester, and the school year.

Just as the skilled server attends and responds to multiple tracks amid the noise and motion of a busy dinner service, master classroom practitioners organize the flow of time and energy towards purposeful outcomes for their

Expertise and Brain Development

Expertise in any field emerges from increasing mental and physical skills. These resources are rooted in brain development. Human thoughts, feelings, and movements surge across the brain as precisely timed electric signals traveling through chains of neurons that form neural networks linked to the original stimulus. A white fatty substance called myelin sheaths these bundles of nerve fibers at they develop. Like insulation on the wiring of a house, the protective myelin wrapping increases the speed, strength, and accuracy of the electrical impulses in the brain. Repeated firings of a neural circuit stimulate additional myelin production. Each new layer increases the fluency and robustness of thoughts and movements (Coyle, 2009).

students and themselves. There are distinct and considerable differences between novice and expert practice and novice and expert thinking. Thinking about mentoring as promoting brain growth for novice teachers means strategically targeting which circuits to fire and re-fire. The templates for planning, reflecting, and problem solving found in Section Three are examples of the thinking circuits that all teachers ignite to power their instructional design and delivery.

Five Spheres of Teaching Expertise

The knowledge base on teaching is both wide and deep. How practitioners organize that knowledge matters. Experts develop mental clusters of interrelated information (Bransford, et al, 1999). Expertise researchers call these clusters chunks (Ericsson & Pool, 2016). These chunks are held in long-term memory, with each cluster having distinctive elements and features that are mentally flagged for ease of retrieval. Experts have more available chunks than non-experts. For example, for expert teachers giving task directions is one chunk. For novices, giving directions includes multiple elements: pacing, intonation, vocabulary choice, use of visuals, and monitoring student understanding.

We are organizing teaching expertise in five spheres: knowledge of the structure of the discipline(s); knowledge of teaching skills and strategies; knowledge of learners and learning; knowledge of self; and knowledge of collaboration. (See Figure 5.1: Five Spheres of Teaching Expertise). These

Figure 5.1 Five Spheres of Teaching Expertise

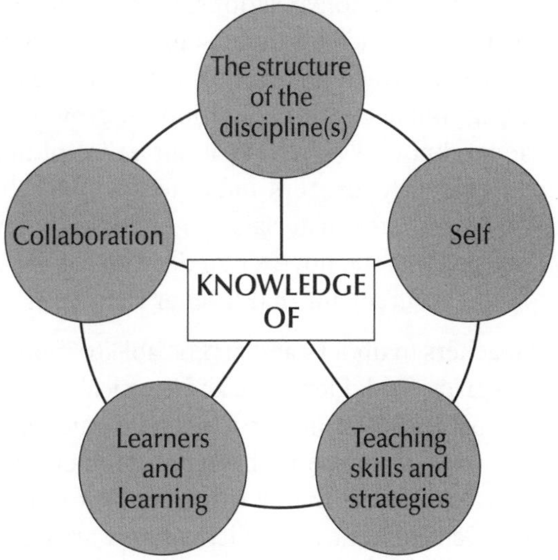

spheres provide frameworks for exploring growth areas for novice teachers. They provide organizers for the mentor to structure learning-focused conversations with a beginning teacher; to set learning goals; and to assemble resources for supporting and sustaining growth in personal and craft knowledge. These spheres are also useful guides for mentors to reflect on their own teaching and collaborative work with other colleagues.

Knowledge of the Structure of the Discipline

Teacher knowledge of the structure of a given content discipline correlates highly with student success in that area. This understanding moves beyond content knowledge alone and into the organization of knowledge within each domain. The structure of the discipline means knowing the big ideas within a content area: the organizing principles, key concepts, and the ways in which they influence one another (Wiggins & McTighe, 2005; Shulman, 1987). These curricular frameworks are delineated in national, state, and provincial standards and serve as an important reference for mentor-novice conversations.

The teacher's deep content understanding greatly influences the design of units and lessons and produces instructional flexibility so that students can develop meaningful cognitive maps of their own (Darling-Hammond & Bransford, 2005). When teachers' understanding is fragmented, they can actually contribute to student misconceptions within that content area. In elementary mathematics, for example, understanding means being able to explain and illustrate a sense of number and how various operations such as addition and subtraction relate to each other. In social studies, it means showing students how to apply geographic, political, historical, economic, and social perspectives to a given situation.

Teachers with rich structural knowledge are more flexible and resourceful in meeting the challenges that arise during classroom lessons. Real learning is messy. Students do not always fit neatly within the boundaries of lesson plans. Therefore, teacher content knowledge must always be greater and more fully integrated than that of their students. This level of understanding allows teachers to prioritize and select the most appropriate content objectives for their students.

During planning and reflecting conversations, mentors need to listen carefully for gaps in a novice teacher's understanding of important curricular ideas. Creating a climate in which it is safe for a novice to ask for help with content understandings is a necessary condition for growth. No one, least of all a beginning teacher, knows everything about a discipline. This is especially true for elementary teachers and others who teach more than one content area. Providing resource materials and including mini-tutorials during conversations reduces the novice's anxiety and at the same time helps to ensure content accuracy for that teacher's students.

It is important for teachers to understand and be able to model the specialized ways of thinking in a given field. Literature and physical science, for example, each have their own principles of inquiry. In social studies, ideas are organized in specific ways. Mathematics has a rich problem solving repertoire. Writing narrative text is different than writing expository text. Each of these ways of knowing is a rich element within its content area. By promoting these skills and perspectives, teachers help students discover how those who produce knowledge and knowing in a specific domain develop and modify ideas. So, too, mentors create these understandings for their beginning teacher.

Each content area is a minefield of misconceptions. Experienced teachers learn to anticipate these as they appear within curriculum topics. Their lesson plans reflect this thinking as they design ways to surface and dispel these barriers to deeper understanding. Knowing which misconceptions are developmentally appropriate at certain stages of learning is valuable craft knowledge. Knowing how to help students work through them is even more useful.

Knowledge of the structure of a discipline is specific to that content area. For example, at the elementary level, this knowledge informs the approach to instruction in reading or mathematics (Snow, Griffin, & Burns, 2005; Hill, Rowan, & Ball, 2005). For secondary teachers, this knowledge usually means specific topics within a curriculum.

For example, one study of first year biology teachers noted that when the novices were presenting topics with which they had great depth of knowledge, they let their classes explore ideas as they asked questions that were more open-ended and promoted richer classroom discourse. When the novices were less confident of their own content knowledge, lessons were structured more rigidly, they talked more than their students, and asked lower cognitive level questions (Carlson, 1993).

A novice's approach to specific subject areas is a special consideration for mentors of both elementary and secondary teachers. The choice of stance—calibrating, consulting, collaborating, or coaching may need to be weighted differently for different content areas or curriculum topics. While beginning teachers encounter a general set of universal challenges, content specific issues need to be analyzed for possible interventions. If classroom management issues crop up at specific times of day, the beginning teacher's comfort with a specific subject area may be a factor to consider.

A mentor's own content knowledge is a factor here as well. We all have our stretch areas. Sharing these with a new teacher communicates a belief in lifelong learning. It is possible that the novice may have content strengths to share with the mentor and can contribute to mutual learning in that manner.

Knowledge of Teaching Skills and Strategies

Expert teachers, like concert violinists, consciously develop their performance repertoires. They assemble and hone micro routines that are combined and applied to fit a wide variety of conditions and settings. Master teachers automatize many routines and basic moves to free cognitive space for more sophisticated sensing of the needs of their learners. Such unconscious competence is the mark of an expert in the classroom. The lack of automaticity with basic moves, such as getting and maintaining student attention, giving clear directions, and establishing routines for smooth classroom transitions, consumes the emotional and physical energy of beginning teachers. This is why these and other areas of basic classroom management are usually the first level of concerns addressed in the mentor-novice relationship. Until these fundamentals are under control, there is often little space for more sophisticated investigations of instructional practice.

Lack of comfort in these arenas blocks the new teacher's openness to ideas and resources that address other areas of teaching practice. It is often useful to front load face-to-face time at the beginning of the school year to share practical strategies and routines that work well in the mentor's own classroom. This is a prime area for initial Idea Banks or to supply a tip-of-the-week.

Content specific pedagogy is an important variable that increases student success (Sadler, et al., 2013; Hill, Rowan & Ball, 2005; Wenglinsky, 2000). Students whose teachers help them to develop higher-order thinking and problem solving skills linked to specific content areas outperform students whose teachers only convey lower-order skills. Mentors support this essential part of the novice to expert journey, often applying a consulting stance when exploring specific teaching techniques.

PEDAGOGICAL CONTENT KNOWLEDGE

The blend of content knowledge, learner knowledge, and teaching knowledge that connects subject matter to targeted learning strategies is called Pedagogical Content Knowledge or PCK (Shulman, 1987). Expert teachers assemble and draw upon a rich collection of analogies, models, memory aids, and explanatory approaches to represent ideas and understandings to their students. They also develop tricks-of-the-trade for helping students grapple willingly with misconceptions and to accept these as part of the learning process. Helping a new teacher anticipate likely misconceptions and sharing instructional solutions is one way that mentors welcome novices to the joys and challenges of teaching and learning in a given content area.

Knowing content and knowing how students learn that content are separate kinds of knowledge. Effective teachers mesh these knowledge and skill sets to produce contextually rich connections for their learners. These teachers represent concepts and content through culturally and developmentally appropriate illustrations, examples, explanations, demonstrations, and engaging learning experiences (See figure 5.2: Pedagogical Content Knowledge). For example, for math instruction, teachers need to be able to calculate correctly and also need to know how to use physical objects, pictures, or diagrams to represent mathematics concepts and procedures. These teachers are able to provide students with appropriate explanations for rules and processes. They analyze students' solutions and explanations to inform

Figure 5.2 Pedagogical Content Knowledge

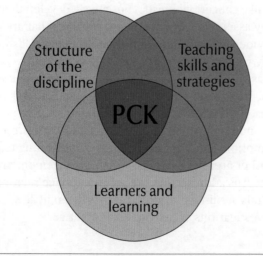

their instruction. When teachers have a clear model of how students learn a specific concept, they can construct learning experiences that help students commit to and test their own ideas. For example, in science instruction, a teacher knowing only the scientific truth appears to have limited effectiveness, particularly if there is a cultural belief that may make acceptance of the scientific view or model difficult.

Knowledge of Learners and Learning

The greatest teaching repertoire in the world is wasted if it is not well matched to the learners' needs (Saphier, Haley-Speca, & Gower, 2018). The changing reality in today's classrooms challenges all teachers, and especially novices. The exploding knowledge base about social and emotional learning, cultural and gender identity, and brain development is central to mentor-novice conversations about producing success for all students.

The push for smaller class sizes and smaller schools is a response to the need to know one another. In an increasingly diverse world, personal knowledge and close relationships connect learners to teachers, to important ideas, and to one another. Teaching students to manage their emotions and behavior, and to make meaningful friendships is as important for school success as cognitive and academic skills. These self-regulation capacities are particularly important for students faced with multiple life-stressors (Shanker, 2017).

Concerns about student discipline, disaffection, lack of commitment, and alienation from school test novice and veterans alike. Proactively supporting new teachers in managing these aspects of classroom work reduces the overall stress load, freeing physical and emotional energy for other important teaching and learning tasks (Zins, et al., 2004).

Given an increasingly diverse student population, the need for culturally respectful approaches to teaching and learning looms large. There are significant discrepancies in both learning outcomes and learning conditions for students who vary by race, culture, language, socioeconomic status, and learning differences. Further, while the student population is increasingly diverse, the teaching force is predominately white, middle class, and female, creating a demographic divide (Gay & Howard, 2000). Thus, most teachers do not have the same cultural frames of reference as their students.

The intrinsically cultural nature of learning and the importance of connecting prior experience to new information makes it critical that teachers understand their students' background and point of view in order to structure meaningful learning experiences for all of them (Lipton & Wellman, 2000). Teachers who approach diversity with a learning mindset are able to be both academically challenging and culturally responsive to students. This orientation and skill set requires a broad base of knowledge that expands and changes as students, contexts, and content shift. This mindset is an important area for emphasis in learning-focused conversations.

Materials and methods that engage one population of learners may confuse or offend another. There is an important overlap here for teachers between this area and knowledge of self. How a teacher came to know an idea or discipline may not be an appropriate or effective cultural match for the students he or she is now teaching that same material.

Language differences are emerging as an important variable for teachers to consider. There is a critical variance between students' social discourse and their formal knowledge of the structure and norms of academic discourse in specific content fields (Lee, et al., 2008). Skilled teachers help students bridge their own language to formal academic language, integrating personal and cultural relevance with content understandings. This learning is more robust and more likely to be retained by students. This concept means that ultimately all teachers, no matter what their content specialties, are teachers of language and teachers of thinking.

"In an increasingly diverse world, personal knowledge, and close relationships connect learners to teachers, to important ideas, and to one another."

Developmental differences extend far beyond the primary grades. Over the years, these differences amplify as the cognitive span between students widens. There are many middle school and high school students who operate at a solid concrete operational level. These learners often run headlong into a curriculum organized by abstractions introduced through symbol systems. When teachers recognize these learning patterns and they approach instruction flexibly, they begin lessons and units with concrete experiences often drawing on students' own life experiences. They then help students represent ideas with pictures and graphics as they support student language development and meaning making. This pathway leads students to firmer conceptual development and richer understandings of abstract ideas and skills integration (Lipton & Wellman, 2000).

Knowledge of Self

Who am I as a learner? What resources can I access/which do I need? Where am I in my own learning journey? What gets in my way?

Mentoring is launching and supporting new teachers on a lifelong journey of professional learning. When mentors are explicit about this goal, they are facilitating a professional vision of the ongoing pursuit of increasing expertise. Knowledge of one's own work style preferences is a special area of self-knowledge. It is important for novice teachers to realize that their preferred style may not be that of all of their students. It is also important for mentors to realize that their own work style may differ from that of their beginning teacher. Some of us perceive and process the world globally. Others prefer more sequential approaches. Some of us are task-driven and others are relationship driven (Lipton & Wellman, 2015). All these style preferences, and the many subtle ways they manifest themselves, appear in our teaching and in the mentor-novice relationship. The ability to stretch against one's own preferred style is a hallmark of the flexibility necessary to connect with a wide variety of learners.

Knowledge of self includes knowledge of the personal values, beliefs, and standards that guide daily decision-making. If teachers are to be effective with an increasingly diverse student population, they need to recognize and understand their own worldviews before they can appreciate and honor the worldviews of their students (McAllister & Irvine, 2000).

Values and beliefs shape the perceptions and judgments that guide teachers through their days. They undergird both personal and student learning goals. Beliefs and values are the most influential element in the type of classroom culture and learning environment that teachers develop with their students (Raths & McAninch, 2003; Pajares, 1992).

Beliefs about the nature of learning and the purposes and process of teaching influence curricular and instructional approaches. These beliefs shape priorities for what students should learn and what and how that is assessed. Beliefs and values can also cause conflict: between new teachers and their colleagues, administrators, parents, and even their own mentors. Conflicting values include: nurturing the child versus pushing for high academic performance; thinking and problem solving versus success on standardized tests; igniting personal passions versus career-readiness; or creating global citizens versus reinforcing local values.

With the press of the clock and calendar, teachers make decisions about what to emphasize and what to let slide. These choices are at heart a matter of values and beliefs. Bringing these to conscious attention helps a beginning teacher address conflicting options and the sometimes conflicting goals encountered when personal beliefs bump headlong into institutional beliefs and values. Mentors can offer support, create cognitive challenge, and facilitate vision in this arena by bringing these values and potential conflicts to consciousness as decision-making tools.

> *"An essential value, and a key component of a professional vision, is that working with others is an important part of a teacher's work, not something that keeps them from their work."*

Knowledge of Collaboration

Knowledge of the whys and hows of collaboration is a key factor of expert practice. Developing expertise in teaching is a joint venture. By participating in communities of practice, new teachers expand and energize their own learning, which in turn enhances the learning of their students. In powerful professional communities, the work of teaching and the craft knowledge for doing it skillfully are collective property. Studies of the best school systems in the world note well-developed patterns of high-quality, collaborative, professional engagement. In these settings, teachers work together to improve their own and others' instructional skills (Barber & Mourshed, 2009). Productive teacher teams regularly gather evidence of students' products and performances and use these data to evaluate and modify instruction to target their students' learning needs (Hattie, 2008).

Successful collaboration requires and develops the knowledge, skills, and dispositions for learning with and from colleagues. This is as true for veterans as it is for beginners. An essential value, and a key component of a professional vision, is that working with others is an important part of a teacher's work, not something that keeps them from their work. In healthy collegial cultures professionals take collective responsibility for all of their students' learning and understand the links to how their own ways of working drive improvements in student performance. Ongoing cycles of assessment, inquiry, analysis, pattern seeking, and planning provide teachers with a fine-grained sense of the cumulative effects of shared practices (Wellman & Lipton, 2017). Mentors prepare and extend their beginning teachers capacities to engage with colleagues in this crucial work.

Expert collaborators have practical knowledge of how adults work and learn together in groups. They know how to contribute to the learning of others and how to develop ideas and resources with their fellow professionals. Productive peer interaction takes courage, especially for beginning teachers as they negotiate the vulnerabilities and insecurities of opening their physical and metaphorical classroom doors to the scrutiny of others. Structuring and supporting the growth of new teachers as collaborative colleagues is a critical mentor responsibility.

A skilled chemistry teacher notices something is not right in her classroom. The noise level and level of student attention to the lab task does not match her sense of what is most appropriate for this lesson. As an expert teacher and expert thinker, she first notices her own awareness, remembering how she might have responded in her first years of teaching. She quickly scans the class to gather additional information to formulate her next decision. She controls the impulse to admonish students for their behavior. The wisdom of experience has taught her that when students are off-task, there might be something wrong with the task itself. These thoughts and the monitoring of these thoughts all occur in split seconds as she mentally sorts out possible issues and possible actions.

Moving to the center of the lab, she calls for a pause in the action and calmly asks selected students to describe the source of their confusion. This action restores a sense of order and purposefulness to the room. By noticing and controlling her thinking, this master teacher is able to resolve this issue and smoothly extend student learning. Had she reacted impulsively, without monitoring and controlling her inner responses, she might have broken the lesson flow by contributing to student distraction and breaking momentum for all involved.

Transitioning from Novice to Expert

Experts think differently about their practice than do novices. Expert teachers are able to operate both in the moment and over time with clear outcomes in mind; skillfully managing students, content, equipment, materials, the clock, and the calendar. They also apply greater complexity and sophistication in analyzing and understanding instructional problems.

One study of the ways novice teachers varied from expert teachers in their thinking about classroom management illuminates the stark difference in the ways the two groups frame issues in their classrooms. The novice teachers thought in terms of maintaining discipline and control. These teachers focused on student compliance and classroom order. The more expert teachers maintained a focus on creating and sustaining a positive learning environment and filtered student behavior and teacher intervention through that goal (Wolff et al., 2015).

The self-talk of experts differs greatly from that of novices. Expert teachers develop and internalize patterns and behaviors that free their attention for the more interactive and dynamic needs of classroom practice. Expert teachers automatize routines for management tasks like taking attendance and focusing students' attention. They have mental scripts for tasks such as monitoring student understanding, varying call and response patterns, and dignifying errors and responding to student misconceptions. Automaticity with these procedures and moves free teachers' mental and physical energy to focus on student learning needs and ways to respond to them (Wiliam, 2016; Berliner, 2001).

Expert teachers access their informed self-talk in a variety of ways, monitoring decisions, choices, and the impact of actions. This is the inner voice of expertise. As they access this resource, master teachers continually sort through their internalized knowledge-bases about the structure of the discipline they are currently teaching, their instructional repertoire, knowledge of the individual students with whom they are working, and knowledge about their own goals, values, and beliefs (See Five Spheres of Teaching Expertise, above). As they sort this treasure-trove of options, master teachers mentally articulate and apply clear criteria for their selections.

> *"Expert teachers are able to operate both in-the-moment and over time with clear outcomes in mind; skillfully managing students, content, equipment, materials, the clock, and the calendar."*

It is the kinds and qualities of their filters that most separates experts from novices. Expert teachers are able to pursue multiple goals for a wider variety of students during the flow of the lesson than are novices. They always have big picture outcomes for thinking and social skills and continually reinforce them. They manage relationships with the whole class at the same time that they intervene with, and support, individual learners. Experts design specific lessons that fit within a bigger curriculum plan that is operating all the time. Beginning teachers tend to be more immediate, intent on managing the flow of a specific lesson plan or controlling student behavior.

Accessing this sophisticated and complex inner voice is the essence of intention-driven action in the classroom. This vital feedback loop helps alert teachers match their choices and behaviors with their intentions, encouraging in-flight reflection and self-monitoring. This attention might mean monitoring the pace of one's speech and use of pauses to elicit student thinking. It also might mean controlling emotions when responding to a difficult student. In essence, it is the thermostat of self-control that regulates attention, task-focus, impulsiveness, humor, and a host of emotional, mental, and physical responses. In the beginning, an experienced colleague's ease of responsiveness may seem unattainable. Without the explanations of a supportive mentor, learning these skills remains elusive. Initially, the voice of the mentor becomes the inner voice of the novice. As novices internalize productive classroom habits they also learn to listen to and trust their own self-talk.

Five Stages of Growth

The quest for expertise in all fields is a developmental process. Mastery is a practice that requires practice. Skilled mentors in all disciplines teach their novices how to practice, and therefore how to learn. Expert teachers described above draw upon a wealth of craft knowledge to plan instruction, solve problems, and analyze their effectiveness. This knowledge is not always explicit; in fact, it may be so well integrated that it seems intuitive to skilled veterans. That the primary source for learning for experienced teachers is, in fact, their own context and content specific experience may not be very encouraging for those new to educational practice. However, the internal scripts and routines of experts can be shared and transferred to novices as beginners receive standards-based feedback and refine their criteria for self-assessment.

Craft knowledge and expertise in teaching take time to acquire. For mentors and beginners alike, it is useful to know that the transition from novice to expert occurs in predictable, measurable stages. David Berliner describes five distinct stages in this journey: novice, advanced beginner, competent, proficient, and expert (Calderhead, 1996).

NOVICE

Novice teachers seek the comfort of rules and procedures for guidance. They seek external guidelines and others' judgments to determine the correctness of their actions. They cling to the comfort of the Teacher's Guide and ask for validation from their mentors regarding their progress. Descriptions become prescriptions, and planning takes the form of preparing the exact lesson presented in the curriculum guide or instructional manual. Initially, there is little variation from the scripted text and scant attention to individual student responses. Their lack of repertoire leads them to duplicate, in the precise sequence, the lesson as planned. They have little capacity for monitoring their class and adjusting the instruction accordingly.

ADVANCED BEGINNER

Advanced beginners start to stretch the pattern a bit. They are in the early stages of developing richer knowledge about basic classroom operations, their students, and teaching specific subjects. Their growing knowledge of the curriculum, the classroom, and their content area increases their confidence to flex. They are better able to season the prescribed lesson plans with strategies of their own, and to adjust the lesson based on student responses. They are comfortable incorporating tips from colleagues and are forming their own preferences in both content and technique.

COMPETENT

Competent teachers have the ability to read student responses and change course to meet learning needs. They are goal-oriented across a spectrum of instructional concerns. They can differentiate instruction both in planning and in implementation. Ongoing assessment of student progress determines lesson design. The teacher's manual no longer controls the instructional decision making.

PROFICIENT

Proficient teachers hold a much larger picture of practice than do teachers at previous stages. They operate at multiple levels simultaneously. They also have a broader temporal horizon, skillfully crafting goals and organizing instruction for both short-term and long-term gains.

Expert

Expert teachers continue to expand personal and professional proficiency in all areas of their teaching. Routines are automatized and attention is freed to interact with learners. There is an organic flow to their day that extends to the ways students self-manage many classroom routines. Teachers at this stage are proactive, anticipating and addressing potential problems before they arise. They have fluidity in applying their wide array of technical knowledge and skills about learning and learners. When problems do emerge, they can generate multiple solutions and make effective choices. While seeing children as unique individuals, their personal catalog of learner types helps them to assemble targeted materials and lessons that smooth learning pathways for all learners. Their capacity to generalize from their rich experience guides their decision making, enabling them to create lessons that target materials and instruction into an organic flow. They cultivate self-managing, self-directed learners.

The development from novice to expert takes many years of experience. While a beginner is still struggling to master basic classroom routines, the effective instructional practices of their mentors may seem unobtainable. To transfer these routines from experienced teacher to novice requires heightened awareness and skill. The need for conscious attention is one of the gifts of mentoring. In order to share and think aloud about the intention behind their actions, experienced practitioners reconnect with and analyze their own repertoire.

Mentoring Across Developmental Stages

According to Berliner, the novice stage occupies the first year of teaching. Most teachers reach the competence stage after three or four years, with only a modest proportion moving to the proficient stage and fewer still attaining expert status. It is important to note that expertise is context specific. Most teachers show steady improvement in the first few years of practice, but student learning gains are greater when their teachers teach the same grade every year (Jacob & Rokoff, 2011). The growth from novice to more expert teaching requires more than simple experience. It is also a highly personal voyage through the seas of professional development. Having a skilled navigator along to plot the course and find safe harbors increases the safety of the journey and allows one to enjoy the adventure. Skilled mentors come equipped with a chart, a compass, and knowledge of the route ahead.

Seven Lenses for Listening

A beginning teacher's developmental stage influences a mentor's decisions regarding the stance to take with a given issue. In both formal and informal interactions, skillful mentors attend to their beginning teacher's language as a way to gain insight into the beginner's current inner voice. How is this new teacher thinking about their content, student goals, instructional strategies, potential choice points, use of data, problem solving, and collaborative practices with colleagues? (See Table 5.1: Seven Lenses for Listening).

Understanding the levels of emerging expertise is a critical knowledge base for effective mentors. These mentors craft interactions that match and stretch the novice's current knowledge and skill. Asking novice teachers questions that are too far beyond their ability to respond may be detrimental to their confidence and to the mentoring relationship. The following seven lenses for listening provide information to growth oriented mentors regarding their novices' present level of development. In this way, mentors can plan strategies to serve needs in-the-moment and over time (See Table 5.2 – 5.8: Mentor Moves for the Seven Lenses).

Table 5:1 Seven Lenses for Listening

Learning-focused Mentors Attend to:	Novice	Emerging Competence	Expert
Depth of content knowledge	Focused on coverage.	Provides vivid, culturally appropriate examples. Maintains flexibility by sorting nice from necessary.	Connects and interweaves concepts and big ideas. Models discipline-based thinking.
Source of goals for lessons and units	Over-reliance on external sources: learning standards, curriculum documents, teacher guides.	Expands beyond content objectives to integrate cognitive and social/emotional outcomes. Establishes both short-and long-term goals.	Derived from an understanding of content matched to individual and collective student learning needs. Targeted towards self-managing, self-directed learners.
Instructional design and delivery	Activity-based planning. Does not deviate from plan during teaching.	Strategies are goal driven, informed by informal and formal assessments, and customized and differentiated to meet student needs.	Applies rich repertoire of instructional scaffolds, analogies, models, and memory-aids.
Ability to recognize and generate choice points	Unaware that there are choice points in lessons. Sticks to the plan, watches the clock.	Envisions success indicators. Plans for what-ifs. Frequent checks for understanding.	Multi-dimensional, in flight adjustments. Wide repertoire of go-to's. Seizes the teachable moment: for the class, small groups, and individual students.
Depth of evidence cited	Data collection is not built into plans. Taps limited sources of data.	Applies multiple measures. Assessment-driven planning.	Wide range of data types and sources. Searches for patterns.
Approaches to problem solving	Focused on immediate solutions. Seeks advice "tell me what to do."	Frames problem before developing solutions.	Takes a balcony view to gain perspective. Frames and reframes problems. Generates multiple possible solutions.
Relationship to professional community	Fearful of self-disclosure. Consumes more than contributes.	Sees collaboration as part of professional responsibilities. Draws from, and contributes to, colleagues' thinking.	Promotes collective responsibility for student learning. Commits to group's goals and growth.

The Depth of Content Knowledge

Expert practitioners have deep knowledge of the structure of the discipline, or disciplines, they teach. They are able to sort the nice from the necessary when developing and applying curricular outcomes to daily instruction. They make critical choices when time is short regarding these distinctions. Lesson plans demonstrate a relationship between what has already been learned and what is expected in future lessons. Skillful teachers also know where to emphasize important and recurring concepts that are foundational to further learning. Expertise in this area includes the ability to articulate connections between large ideas in the curriculum and to support students in making those connections.

As mentors attend fully to their colleagues, they listen to determine to what degree does the new teacher:

- Understand the knowledge, skills, and concepts in the lesson or unit
- Articulate the connections between ideas in the curriculum
- Employ culturally and contextually relevant examples to illustrate the content/concepts

Table 5.2 Mentor Moves for the Seven Lenses: Depth of Content Knowledge

Depth of Content Knowledge		
Novice focuses on coverage: replicates lesson plans from teacher's guide, there is a lack of connection between big ideas, and uses limited examples to illuminate content.		
Mentor Move	**What is it?**	**Might look/sound like**
Ask a coaching question	A question designed to support connection-making between pieces of content and increase awareness of student's relationship to the content that also provides an assessment for the mentor.	*"In this lesson, what are the most critical content understandings you want to teach?"* or *"What are some connections between the content of this lesson and the larger concepts of the unit?"*
Provide a what, why, and how for relevant examples followed by a shift to a collaborating stance	A consulting strategy that offers ideas and the rationale for ideas which prime the pump for co-generation.	*"For your unit on simple machines, you can bring in pictures of household items such as levers, pulleys, wedges, and so on. This is important because providing rich examples that students can relate to increases understanding and retention. You might do this with an online image search, or a kitchen supply catalogue and some cutting and pasting. The cards could then be used for a sorting and classifying strategy or a matching game. Let's consider that as a starter and generate some additional examples for later in the unit."*
Use content standards as a third point, calibrate to the standard and then shift to a coaching stance and inquire	Clarifying the expected standard with specific examples and then inquiring to support more expert thinking about the standard achievement.	*"At this grade level, students are expected to understand the connection between simple machines and the concepts of force, motion, and work. The big idea is that a simple machine conserves energy and makes work easier. What are some ways this standard relates to what you've taught and where you're headed?"*

- Recognize the place of a specific lesson/unit in the larger frame of the curriculum
- Describe the thinking habits within a discipline

The Source of Goals for Lessons and Units

As expertise develops, teachers move from strict adherence to the teachers' guide, or other external sources, to their own understanding of the content and students' needs to determine learning goals. The confident marriage of learning standards to source materials when goal-setting is a developmental indicator. In addition, setting learning goals that nest short-term objectives within longer-term outcomes, connecting the specific lesson or unit to the broader conceptual understandings of the curriculum or content area are indicators of growing expertise. So, too, are goals that include specific thinking skills, or clusters of thinking skills, such as problem solving or decision making; and social skills, such as listening to other points of view or engaging productively in a group task.

As mentors attend fully to their colleagues, they listen to determine to what degree the new teacher:

- Relies on external sources, such as curriculum guides and learning standards to set goals
- Sets both group and individual goals

Table 5.3 Mentor Moves for the Seven Lenses: Source of Goals for Lessons and Units

Source of Goals for Lessons and Units		
Novice establishes goals primarily from external sources.		
Mentor Move	**What is it?**	**Might look/sound like**
Ask a coaching question	A question designed to expand the sources for goal setting and increase the integration of other types of goals (e.g., social/emotional or cognitive processes).	*"In addition to the content objectives, what other outcomes do you want your students to take away from this lesson?"* or *"As you consider the ways you want your students to process this content, what are some specific thinking skill goals you might build-in?"*
Offer a principle of practice, then shift to a collaborating stance	A consulting strategy that provides the conceptual why that is fundamental as a basis for stimulating partnered thinking.	*"It's important that goals target both short-and long-term outcomes. Let's think about a sequence for learning goals in this upcoming unit."*
Use district curriculum documents as a third point, calibrate to the unit goals and then shift to a coaching stance and inquire	Illustrating and clarifying that content goals connect to other learning outcomes. Providing specific examples and then inquiring to support more expert thinking about developing integrated goals.	*"Notice that in this reading lesson, the content goal is about characterization, and the thinking skill goals include compare/contrast and inferential reasoning."* *"What are some social skill goals that might be integrated by using partners for this lesson?"*

- Integrates content goals with social/emotional and cognitive goals
- Sets and manages both short and long term goals

Instructional Design and Delivery

Designing strategies to meet specific outcomes, and modifying them to differentiate for individual learners is an expert skill. A mindful mentor listens to determine whether the beginning teacher is applying instructional methods strategically, or simply activity thinking. The former is a purposeful application, based on the assessment of learner needs, the latter, something found in a teaching journal, sourcebook, or the classroom next door that seems interesting.

As mentors attend fully to their colleagues, they listen to determine to what degree the new teacher:

- Engages in activity-based planning
- Draws on a rich repertoire of instructional strategies
- Has clear criteria for choosing instructional strategies
- Customizes and differentiates chosen strategies

Table 5.4 Mentor Moves for the Seven Lenses: Instruction Design and Delivery

Instructional Design and Delivery		
Novice engages in activity-based planning and does not deviate while teaching.		
Mentor Move	**What is it?**	**Might look/sound like**
Ask a coaching question	A question designed to highlight the relationship between the choice of strategy and learning goal or goals and student readiness.	*"Given what you know about your students at this point, how will this strategy build on their present skills?"* or *"What are some criteria you use to determine which instructional strategies will be most effective?"*
Think aloud about how you match strategies to goals, and then shift to a collaborative stance to co-generate additional criteria for choosing instructional strategies	Modeling an expert's self-talk regarding instructional design and highlighting the need for criteria-based planning.	*"When I think about strategy choice, one criteria for me is student learning goals. So, I mentally scan my options, then consider student learning goals and readiness to find the best match. Let's brainstorm additional criteria that make sense to you for strategy choice."*
Use the standard for effective planning as a third point and calibrate to the rubric descriptions, such as effective use of materials and resources, then shift to a coaching stance and inquire	Clarifying a standard with context specific examples, then inquiring to expand the new teacher's thinking about effective implementation of the standard, then inquiring to expand the novice's thinking about criteria for choosing strategies.	*"As the standard indicates, instructional materials and strategies need to appropriately match the learning needs of your students. Based on your sense of student readiness, what are some ways you determine strategy choice?"*

The Ability to Recognize and Generate Choice Points

For skillful teachers, clear intentions regarding learning outcomes drive instructional choices. As proactive planners, these teachers incorporate if-then thinking to build in potential contingencies in a lesson or unit of study. When implementing planned choices, including instructional objectives, learning materials, interaction and grouping patterns, and time management, these teachers consistently monitor their effectiveness. They make adjustments to meet the immediate needs of the learners, while being mindful of the larger instructional picture. The ability to draw from repertoire to make in-the-moment refinements or revisions to the initial plan is a hallmark of expertise.

As mentors attend fully to their colleagues, they listen to determine to what degree the new teacher:

- Describes the need to modify instruction based on observations of student behavior
- Considers what-ifs types during the planning processes
- Embeds checks for understanding in lesson plans

Table 5.5 Mentor Moves for the Seven Lenses: Ability to Recognize and Generate Choice Points

Ability to Recognize and Generate Choice Points		
The novice identifies limited options for choice while planning or teaching.		
Mentor Move	What is it?	Might look/sound like
Ask a coaching question	A question designed to increase awareness of the need to anticipate choice points.	*"As you think about this lesson, what are some predictions about places where you might need a plan B?"*
Offer a menu and then shift to a collaborating stance	A consulting strategy that expands instructional repertoire and offers potential options that establishes readiness for co-determining pros and cons about each one.	*"Given the need to determine whether you need to modify your plan, there are several ways you might check for students' understanding in this math lesson: a signal like thumbs up/thumbs down; ask a question and randomly select responders; or have students write a response and hold up mini white boards. Let's consider the pros and cons for each of these techniques based on what you know about your students."*
Use the teaching standard for effective instruction as a third point and calibrate to the rubric descriptions, such as adjusting the lesson based on student responses; then shift to a coaching stance and inquire	Clarifying a standard with context specific examples, then inquiring to expand the new teacher's thinking about effective implementation of the standard; then inquiring to develop increased awareness regarding flexibility and responsiveness before and during instruction.	*"This standard is based on the need to be poised to modify a plan at any point, and to be a proactive planner for that contingency. What are some ways that you determine whether students are with you or you need to flex?"*

Depth of Evidence Cited

Effective teaching requires the application of day-to-day and moment-to-moment assessment of student learning to inform future action. Expert teachers draw upon a wide range of data sources for planning and reflecting upon learning. Possibilities include text-based inventories, student work products, teacher-made tests, classroom observation of student behaviors, learner interviews, and inventories, all of which are rich resources for determining short and long term next steps – for individual students, groups of students, and the class as a whole.

As mentors attend fully to their colleagues, they listen to determine to what degree the new teacher:

Builds data collection into lesson plans

- Draws on multiple measures to determine student progress
- Engages in assessment driven planning and reflecting
- Searches for and acts upon patterns in the data

Table 5.6 Mentor Moves for the Seven Lenses: Depth of Evidence Cited

Depth of Evidence Cited		
The novice taps limited sources of data to guide planning and instructional decision making.		
Mentor Move	**What is it?**	**Might look/sound like**
Ask a coaching question	A question designed to increase awareness about assessment driven planning and reflecting, and to increase the repertoire of options for formative and summative assessments.	*"What are some methods for determining student progress that are built into this lesson?" or "What types of student work products might you combine with in-class observation to increase your confidence in student progress?"*
Refer to research regarding formative assessment, and shift to a collaborating stance to co-design applications	A consulting strategy that presents a research-based rationale for effective action and sets the stage for collaboratively generating practical ways to apply these findings.	*"Current research indicates that formative assessment is one of the most powerful influences on student learning success. Frequent checks for understanding are an important part of this process. Let's design some formative assessments for your next lesson."*
Use the standard on using assessment in instruction as a third point, calibrate to the rubric descriptions then shift to a coaching stance and inquire	Clarifying a standard with context specific examples, then inquiring to expand the new teacher's thinking about ways to monitor student learning.	*"This standard addresses the importance of continuous monitoring of student learning. In your class, that would mean identifying the types of data that would most help you determine learning successes and challenges for all students. What might be some ways to gather formative assessment information using student work products in your upcoming lessons?"*

Approaches to Problem Solving

Expert problem solvers spend the bulk of their energy defining the problem before seeking solutions. They understand that both problem definition and clear success indicators set the direction for productive resolution. Expert problem solvers can step outside of the immediate situation to access emotional resourcefulness, gain perspective on patterns and causal factors, and seek multiple solutions. These capacities contribute to their confidence and ability to effectively resolve challenging issues.

As mentors attend fully to their colleagues, they listen to determine to what degree the new teacher:

- Seeks advice rescue/advice for solutions
- Seeks immediate solutions to ill-defined problems
- Engages in problem-framing/reframing before developing solutions

Table 5.7 Mentor Moves for the Seven Lenses: Approaches to Problem Solving

Approaches to Problem Solving		
The novice seeks quick solutions, often from others, before defining the problem.		
Mentor Move	What is it?	Might look/sound like
Ask a coaching question	A question designed to shift the novice's energy to define the problem before generating solutions.	*"What's your hunch about what might be triggering these behaviors?"* or *"What are some patterns you're noticing about when these behaviors occur?"*
Offer potential causal factors and then shift to a collaborating stance	A consulting strategy that shifts energy to problem causes rather than problem fixes and provides a context for a paired conversation about the most likely causes prior to seeking solutions.	*"So, you're finding that many of your students can't accurately measure materials in your chemistry labs. Some possible factors that might be causing this problem are: not knowing how to read the scales; not correctly transferring their readings to the lab sheets; or because they have no idea why accuracy matters. Let's consider which of these, if any, are the most likely causes."*
Inquire to determine the scope and scale of the problem	A question intended to determine how the novice is presently framing the problem and to gather more specific information about the parameters.	*"When you say accurate measurement, what percentage of your students are struggling with this skill?"*

Relationship to Professional Community

Being a contributing member of a vital learning community is an important professional responsibility. Teachers who seek collaboration and draw from and contribute to their colleagues' thinking are valued members of a learning culture. These teachers are committed to the group's goals, share responsibility for all students' learning, and identify themselves as part of a group that is continuously improving.

As mentors attend fully to their colleagues, they listen to determine to what degree the new teacher:

- Limits participation due to fear of self-disclosure
- Draws from and contributes to colleagues' thinking
- Expresses commitment to the group's goals and growth
- Shares responsibility for all students' learning

Table 5.8 Mentor Moves for the Seven Lenses: Relationship to Professional Community

Relationship to Professional Community		
The novice expresses concern about ways to participate in team meetings and seems fearful of self-disclosure.		
Mentor Move	**What is it?**	**Might look/sound like**
Ask a coaching question	A question designed to increase the new teacher's value for being a participating team member.	*"What are some of the things you're noticing about participating as a team member?"*
Offer a perspective shift related to team work and then shift to a collaborative stance	A consulting strategy that offers another way of thinking about working as a team member that leads to a shared exploration of both the challenges and rewards of professional community.	*"It's possible that your colleagues don't want to put any pressure on you and so they carry most of the weight in team meetings. Let's brainstorm some ways you might indicate your interest and readiness for greater participation."*
Use the teaching standard on professional community as a third point, calibrate to the rubric descriptions and then shift to a coaching stance and inquire	Clarifying a standard with context specific examples, then inquiring to increase the teacher's confidence in participating more fully as a team member.	*"The standard for high performance as a team member describes the importance of contributing to the shared work of improving practice. When you think of opportunities to do that with your team, what are some things that come to mind?"*

Choosing Stance

An attuned mentor balances her approach as she navigates across the continuum of interaction; calibrating, consulting, collaborating, and coaching as is most appropriate to support the developmental needs of her colleague. The hardest call is knowing when to remain in a coaching stance to support the novice's struggle through difficult decision making processes rather than solving the problems for her. By appreciating these instances as developmental differences, we are then able to seize the teachable moment and support learning and growth in a meaningful way.

The quality of the novice's responses determine the mentor's choice of stance. If responses seem partially complete, or if the mentor has specific information to add, a collaborative stance will facilitate the generation of rich information built upon the novice's presenting knowledge base. When the response indicates a lack of knowledge or information, a consultative stance, which includes the key principles of practice related to the issue, a framework for thinking about the topic, a think aloud that makes the mentor's expert processing visible to the novice, and/or a menu of suggestions will fill the immediate gaps and support future learning.

Mentoring as a Professional Vision

As mentors gain experience and perspective on the craft of mentoring, they gain new insights into themselves as teachers and as learners. This learning occurs on multiple levels. On one level, mentors develop richer understandings about the craft of teaching. While engaging in personal reflection and articulating their own knowledge base to novices, they deepen and integrate personal knowledge about professional practice. On another level, mentors revisit their own history as teachers as they monitor the growth of their new colleagues and come to see the parallel between this journey and the journey all learners take in any new field of endeavor. Yet on another level, the mentor is learning about the art of supporting novice teachers. This, too, becomes a voyage of discovery in the passage from novice to expert mentoring.

"*We need to embrace the idea that teaching is a set of skills that can be taught and learned and constantly improved upon. . . But what's happened in sports over the past forty years teaches that the way to improve how you perform is to improve the way you train. High performance isn't, ultimately, about running faster, throwing harder, or leaping farther. It's about something much simpler: getting better at getting better.*"

— James Surowiecki

SECTION 6 | Strategies for Success

T HE strategies shared in the following pages are practical extensions and enhancements of the mentoring relationship. As these tips and tricks require varying investments of time and resources, they are organized by degree of effort required for implementation. They range from minimal time and energy to moderate investments to more extensive commitments. Additionally, these useful strategies are organized by most appropriate time of year for application. Some ideas are great for the beginning or end of the school year, while others may be ongoing. You may want to correlate these ideas with the Calendar of Options in Section 1: The Mentor As Growth Agent.

MEET, GREET, AND SHARE

Purpose: *To connect beginning teachers with the faculty in a way that addresses both personal and professional needs.*

Schedule a brief meeting before or after school for grade level/content area personnel. Ask each attendee to bring two things to the meeting: a funny classroom memory and a favorite teaching resource. While sharing snacks and beverages, take the opportunity to share favorite resources as well as memorable experiences. This exchange provides the beginning teacher with additional resource ideas, reinforces a collegial school culture, and attends to affective needs as well.

Extensions

- Capture resources and stories in a journal for future reference and sharing.

- Each member prepares an index card describing "What I know now that I wish I had known then."

- Use the Meet, Greet, and Share for a mentor and/or beginning teacher support group meeting.

Tips

Include beginning teachers in sharing memories and resources from pre-service experiences.

Pace the meeting to ensure appropriate time for discussion of resources including how and when they have been used, practical tips for use, and where and how to locate them.

WELCOME TO. . . BASKET

Purpose: *To provide the beginning teacher with items that are useful but may be forgotten in routine preparations. To establish connections between the beginning teacher and existing faculty.*

Construct a Welcome To (school name) Basket filled with useful personal and professional items. Invite colleagues to provide items for the basket as appropriate. Suggested items include:

- Post-it notes
- Pens
- Thumb drive with tips, strategies, and other teaching aids
- A coupon book with free services such as one lunch duty, assistance with paperwork, etc.
- Throat lozenges
- Tissues
- Instructional books or journals
- Snacks
- A box of colored chalk
- Item with school insignia, such as a school poster, T-shirt or coffee mug.

Extensions

- As a faculty, construct a list of Top Ten Things you need or need to know and include in all Welcome To. . . Baskets. This interaction also serves as an interactive, collegial activity for staff.
- With colleagues, design a Red Letter Dates calendar to include in the baskets. In addition to traditional dates, these calendars might indicate vacations, staff social events, cultural events in the community, theater offerings too good to miss and other renewal activities.
- Design different baskets for experienced teachers who are new to the district concentrating more on their specific needs in the new assignment.

Tip

Keep the contents of the basket light and somewhat fanciful as a break from what might be an overwhelming amount of instructional and logistical information at the beginning of the year.

Beginning of Year | Minimal Effort

NEW TEACHER LUNCHEON/SHOWER

Purpose: *To acquaint new staff with existing staff and community resources. This event promotes collegiality and allows for personal and professional relationship building.*

Plan a luncheon or shower for all new teachers. This group should include novices and experienced teachers who are new to the school (or district), as well as staff transferred from within the system. For a luncheon, plan a covered dish or a box lunch. A shower might be held after school with snacks.

Include in the luncheon or shower goodie bags or gift boxes that might contain items such as:

- Coupon book where you have assembled discounts for local businesses, free soft drink, or other snacks. Copy of the previous year's annual or yearbook to be used to match faces with names.

- School insignia items such as T-shirt, coffee mugs, or canvas bags.

- Map of the school with a listing of personnel and assignments including specialized support and committees.

- Highlighted and annotated handbook of policies, procedures, and regulations.

- Items for the classroom such as bulletin board border, timer, patterns or templates for instructional materials, and pens/pencils.

Extensions

- Invite parents, members of the community, and business representatives.

- Include maps of the local area and locations of other schools in the gifts and goodies.

- Invite staff to bring a grab bag item with a concealed item to be swapped with other staff so each person leaves with something.

Tips

Coordinate the event to ensure that each staff person leaves with a goodie.

Organize activities during the luncheon/shower that serve as getting-to-know you or, for existing staff, getting-to-know you better energizers.

Plan for opportunities to highlight parents, business, and community members that are present. Provide time for sharing and exchanging information and resources with them.

Moderate Effort   Beginning of Year

JOINT PLANNING SESSION

Purpose: *To collaboratively plan for the first week of school.*

Ideally, this session is held at least two weeks prior to the beginning of the school year. Additional planning sessions may be held at the beginning of the second semester or at any point when a need or desire arises for collaborative planning. The Planning Template may be used to structure conversations regarding lessons or segments of instruction (See Section 2: Structured Conversations: Maximizing Time and Attention).

- Schedule a minimum of 60 minutes of uninterrupted time. Jointly discuss and plan for the first day of school.
- Collaboratively plan for physical arrangement of the room, instructional displays, use of funds that may be provided by the district for materials, etc.
- Review curriculum requirements.
- Explore instructional plans for the first week of school.

Extensions

- Use the Joint Planning Session to establish professional and personal goals as well as student goals.
- Open the Planning Session to include grade level/content area staff.
- If possible, conduct separate planning sessions for management issues and instructional issues.

Tips

Allot portions of time during the session to share information perceived as critical for beginning the year and to surface questions/concerns of the beginning teacher.

Be attentive to balancing information with time for processing and application.

Schedule subsequent sessions for addressing questions that will emerge from the implementation of plans.

INCREDIBLE IDEAS SCRAPBOOK

Purpose: *To efficiently provide beginning teachers with classroom-tested ideas and resources.*

The Scrapbook may be assembled prior to the beginning of the school year and supplemented at the beginning of the second semester as the mentor continues to collect strategies. Ask colleagues to submit donations to the scrapbook as well. Possibilities to include are:

- Teaching stories
- Poems
- Cartoons
- Tips for remembering student names
- Index cards with strategies for grouping students, learning-center activities, etc.
- Bulletin board display ideas

Extensions

- Extend the scrapbook to include instructional ideas, assessment strategies, and website references.
- Categorize the ideas by content area, time of year, state standard, etc. Develop the scrapbook as a grade level or content area collaborative project.
- Create a book of archetypes illustrating state or district standards. Ask the beginning teacher to add to the ideas and share with others.

Tips

Ideas and suggestions should include type of application, time required, do's and don'ts for successful implementation.

Identify the contributor of each idea to allow for follow-up questions.

Extensive Effort

Beginning of Year

PROFESSIONAL PORTFOLIOS

Purpose: *To establish clear expectations and connect the mentoring relationship to professional standards.*

Using state or district standards, conduct a goal setting conversation which is concrete, specific, and lays out plans for achieving goals, as well as evidence that will support the beginning teacher's self-assessment.

Apply the Planning Template to this interaction, and keep a record of the goals as reference for future conversations.

Begin a portfolio as an ongoing source of self-assessment and reference for continued conversations (See Section 7: Downloadable Resources). Portfolio items might include:

- Sample lesson plans
- Samples of student work
- Pictures of bulletin board displays or learning center items and artifacts created for classroom lessons, letters, and comments from parents
- Reflections and anecdotes from the beginning teacher's journal.

Extensions

- Encourage your beginning teacher to keep a reflective journal (See Section 7: Downloadable Resources). As the portfolio is developed, select items might be included.
- Collaborate with your beginning teacher by keeping a Double-Entry Journal. Your beginning teacher enters thoughts, ideas, concerns, and questions in the left-hand column (or on the left page of the book) and leaves it for you. You enter responses on the opposite side.
- Keep a professional portfolio of your own and share entries and insights.

Tips

Create an organizing scheme for the portfolio. Limit the number of items to 4-6 a month.

Be sure the items in the portfolio relate to the goals established at the beginning of the year. Review the portfolio as a method for reflecting on these goals.

Ongoing   Minimal Effort

GOT IT/NEED IT

Purpose: *To efficiently manage resources and provide optimal access to sometimes limited materials or equipment.*

Post a chart or worksheet in the library, staff room, or Professional Nook (See page 108).

Ask staff members to record items they are willing to share in the Got It column and items needed in the Need It column.

Date	Got It	Need It	Date

Extensions

- Post this information at staff meetings and provide a brief period of time to update.
- Place this information online to encourage sharing among schools.

Tips

Include items purchased by the school or found in the library on the chart to increase communication about resources among staff.

Identify a point person to keep the chart updated.

Use the most requested items, or most used items, as data for future purchasing decisions.

Minimal Effort | Ongoing

LIVELY LIFELINES

Purpose: *To capitalize on support resources for the beginning teacher. To encourage networking.*

Assist the beginning teacher in networking with other professionals by:

- Locating someone to serve as a phone-a-friend resource when a question that must be answered immediately arises.
- Soliciting volunteers to participate as e-mail partners to provide information, forward pertinent correspondence, etc.
- Identifying a go-to mentor that may be in close proximity to the beginning teacher's classroom and may serve as a substitute mentor as needed.
- Introducing the beginning teacher to other professionals and assisting with networking. Acquainting the beginning teacher with the teacher center and other district-based resources.

Extensions

- Include agencies and professionals in the community in the networking process.
- Use technology to network with online resources, including appropriate apps and social media.
- Encourage membership in professional organizations.

Tips

Check with the beginning teacher periodically to ensure communication lines are working.

Include contacts for logistical and clerical assistance, as well as instructional resources.

PROFESSIONAL NOOK

Purpose: *To provide a mechanism for sharing up-to-date literature, research, newsletters and other important and interesting information. To provide a conducive space for professional reading.*

Establish a comfortable space in the faculty room, school library, or other appropriate area for a reading corner. Strategically select the location for minimal traffic and noise if possible. Consider aesthetics by providing lighting, seating, and a table to hold items. Possible sources of reading materials include:

- Professional reading such as journals or recent books, donated graduate school and higher education resources.
- Current magazine articles that may have been highlighted by a previous reader.
- Display of trade samples.
- School newsletters.
- System memorandums.

Extensions

- Ask beginning teachers to donate readings and materials from recent and continuing studies.
- Develop Professional Nooks for each grade level, grade clusters, or department.
- Organize reading materials that focus on a current local initiative.
- Arrange for study groups to meet periodically (e.g., once per month) and cluster reading around the study group's topic.

Tips

Refresh these materials often so information does not become stale.

Ask for a volunteer, possibly the library media specialist, to oversee the ongoing project.

Moderate Effort   Ongoing

PROBLEM SOLVING PARTNERSHIP

Purpose: *To reinforce norms of collaborative problem solving.*

Find opportunities for both the mentor and beginning teacher to share expertise and satisfy mutual or individual needs.

- Designate a meeting when each person will bring a presenting problem or issue to the table. Discuss and surface the desired outcome for one of the presenting problems.
- Brainstorm options for reaching the desired outcome (brainstorming encourages creativity by removing judgment).
- Mutually discuss criteria for selecting action options. Repeat this process, as time allows, for each participant.

Extensions

- Use Problem Solving Partnerships as a grade level, department, or staff meeting activity. Schedule time at a subsequent meeting to update and discuss progress, additional decisions, questions, etc.
- Apply this strategy with students for teaching problem solving skills. Include in mentor and/or beginning teacher support group meetings.
- Extend problem solving to "what happens if?" sessions.

Tips

Attend to pacing during the meeting to make sure each partner shares.

Begin with the mentor's problem to ease anxiety and model lifelong learning.

Ongoing | Extensive Effort

COLLABORATIVE ROLE-ALIKE SUPPORT GROUPS

Purpose: *To provide ongoing support for both beginning teachers and mentors and feedback for assessing the mentoring program.*

Both mentors and beginning teachers need structured opportunities to collaboratively problem solve, seek guidance, and provide mutual support. Convening each group separately allows for enhanced learning and increased effectiveness in the mentoring relationship. It is also important to be time efficient during the meetings. Suggestions for structuring these include:

- Conduct meetings quarterly.
- Include an entry in reflection journals at the beginning of each meeting.
- Structure some reflection prompts to surface issues, concerns, successes, and constructive suggestions for refining the program.
- Provide at least one new idea, strategy, or tool that can be implemented immediately (include content regarding educational practice).
- Reserve a portion of time (minimum of 15 minutes) for trio problem-solving, allowing each member of the trio to state a presenting problem and request consulting, collaborating, or coaching from the remaining members.
- Provide written communication updating events, policy changes, logistical information, etc.

Extensions

- Design support groups for experienced administrators, beginning administrators, and assistants.
- Survey participants periodically to determine burning issues for discussion.

Tips

Allow written communication to speak for itself and clarify when needed.

Pace the meetings according to the agenda and participant needs.

Extensive Effort

Ongoing

COLLABORATIVE STAFF DEVELOPMENT

Purpose: *To promote team planning and implementation of content-driven staff development sessions.*

Collaborative interactions and reciprocal learning are value-added components of the mentoring relationship. Considering district initiatives and mutual foci for growth, identify a staff development opportunity to attend together. Following the staff development, reflect on the learnings and decide on strategies for implementation. Jointly agree on assessment methods and data collection. Also, use the Planning and Reflecting Templates to guide learning-focused conversations. (See Section 2: Structured Conversations: Maximizing Time and Attention).

Extensions

- Jointly assess results from data collection and formulate conclusions. Share results with grade level, content area, and other faculty members.

- Pair with a mentor/beginning teacher team at another school to compare strategies, results, and successes. This active sharing increases the knowledge base for all.

- Plan and implement an integrated project of mutual interest.

Tips

Remember to include tips, adaptations, and important things to remember when sharing results with other professionals.

Use student feedback in refining, revising, and reporting on your work.

| End of Year | Minimal Effort |

PACKING UP

Purpose: *To collectively prepare for the closing of school and an informal opportunity to reflect and debrief on the year's experiences.*

The mentor and beginning teacher jointly plan and complete activities to close the school year. The time spent working together may also be used as a time for sharing and wondering in an informal way. The mentoring partnership may complete some or all of these activities for both rooms:

- Jointly organize materials and supplies.
- Prepare for end-of-year reports such as attendance, inventory, and resource allocation.
- Discuss and complete student reports such as grades, cumulative records, and library records.
- As you work, think out loud regarding learnings from this year. Engage in conversations about expectations for next year's assignment.

Extensions

- Develop or update checklists to guide end-of-year activities.
- Involve grade-level or content area teams in this process.

Tips

Implement as a collaborative activity allowing the beginning teacher the opportunity to be on equal footing as much as possible.

Encourage the beginning teacher to share exciting or interesting ideas and strategies that were particularly successful.

Moderate Effort

End of Year

CELEBRATE SUCCESS

Purpose: *To recognize individual and staff efforts and successes. To share and spread effective ideas. To acknowledge professional and personal efforts.*

You may choose to celebrate projects, partnerships, initiative implementations, and other noteworthy accomplishments by:

- Reminding mentors to share positive accomplishments of beginning teachers with others.
- Highlighting collaborative projects by mentor partnerships in a school newsletter, bulletin board, or staff meeting.
- Constructing a Wall of Fame in a school hallway, workroom or library. This wall could contain pictures and notes regarding accomplishments and efforts by individuals, groups, grade levels, beginning teachers, mentors, and other staff.
- Setting aside time at the last staff meeting of the year to highlight staff accomplishments by grade level.

Extensions

- Include these successes in parent newsletters and at parent meetings such as PTA or PTO.
- Include a Wall of Fame for the system at a school board meeting.
- Recognize collaborative projects that involve staff from more than one school in a special section of the Wall of Fame, newsletter, or bulletin boards.

Tip

Ask both staff and students to nominate distinguished colleagues at designated times throughout the year; perhaps in October, January, March, and May. This practice allows for a variety of activities throughout the year, not just at the end.

AHA CHART

Purpose: *To efficiently capture and share reflections and learnings for both beginning teachers and mentors.*

Ask beginning teachers to complete an Aha chart or log to be shared with future beginning teachers. This technique reinforces the notion of continuing to learn from our experiences and collectively increasing the professional knowledge base.

	Beginning of Year	Middle of Year	End of Year
I am glad I knew . . .			
I wish I had known . . .			
I am still wondering . . .			

Extensions

- Complete the chart for at least the first two years of service.
- Ask mentors to complete the chart regarding their mentoring experience. Use the I am still wondering. . . stem as data for providing information and resources in the future.

Tips

Collect, synthesize, and distribute a summary chart for other staff.

Include this activity during Collaborative Role-Alike Support Group meetings (See page 110) at appropriate times of the year to ensure time for reflection.

LEARNING AT ALL LEVELS

Purpose: *To encourage collaboration among both students and staff.*

This strategy invites the beginning teacher and mentor to collaboratively plan a project or unit for completion by students in each classroom.

- Brainstorm possible projects or units that would be of high interest and directly relate to student outcomes. Devise a plan of action, identifying resources, responsibilities, timelines, and other staff that might be needed or involved.
- Prepare students for the project and the collaborative activities. At the end of the project, jointly celebrate the results.

Extensions

- Debrief the project at several levels; learning from the project (students and staff) and learning from working with each other.
- Plan a joint field trip to enhance the learning.

Tip

Choose a unit or topic of high interest to both colleagues and students. Select a topic that allows the beginning teacher to contribute equally.

TIPS TOO GOOD TO LEAVE OUT

Just a few more ideas too good to leave out, organized as timesavers, learning opportunities, relationship builders, and additional support.

Timesavers

- Provide printed regulations, policies, and procedures with highlights or annotations. Suggest that your beginning teacher keep an ongoing list of questions/needs in her classroom. Jointly construct a calendar with red letter days and high jam periods.

- Order supplies before they are needed.

- Anticipate likely concerns and problems. Create a life-saver file of practical ideas to address them.

Learning Opportunities

- Provide small amounts of information as needed. Avoid doing an information dump.

- Plan for Problem Solving Partners Sessions (at least 3 per year) where each person has a presenting problem and you jointly engage in brainstorming, assessing options, and decision-making (See page 109).

- Seek opportunities to collaborate with your beginning teacher and arrange for observation opportunities.

- Arrange for practice assessment observations by a peer or the mentor to familiarize the beginning teacher with the process.

- Model teaching procedures and think aloud with the beginning teacher about your choice points, criteria for selecting strategies, and personal learnings from a teaching experience.

- Duplicate and share resource files containing ideas and activities for activating and integrating content.

Relationship Builders

- Mentors should share challenges faced and strategies used to overcome barriers. Conduct a conference while taking a walk, sitting outside, etc. to reduce stress. Model trustworthy behavior/confidentiality.

- Attend to stress management strategies. Develop common and shared vocabulary.

- Seek opportunities to grow together and move across the continuum from consultant to coach.

Additional Support

- Leave notes of encouragement and support, particularly during the first two weeks of school and during times of intensive paperwork/reporting requirements.

- Trade professional articles of interest, highlight important points first. Accompany beginning teacher on the first non-teaching assignment.

- Introduce beginning teacher to support services staff and provide information on available services. Assist with identifying special needs students in the beginning teacher's classroom.

SECTION 7 | Downloadable Resources

This section includes thumbnails of downloadable forms including: self-assessment rubrics for the mentoring relationship, personal mentoring skills, and beginning teacher needs; time-saving quick forms for focusing mentor/novice communication; and structured pages for beginning teacher reflection. You'll also find tools for establishing and monitoring a growth plan, enhancing learning from the text, and exercises to stretch your mentoring skills using video.

You will find files on our website **www.miravia.com/resources/mentoring-matters** for each of these forms organized as follows:

DOWNLOAD THESE FORMS AT:

www.miravia.com/resources/ mentoring-matters

Formative and Self-Assessment Tools

Mentors, beginning teachers, and their developing relationships benefit from ongoing assessment. These forms structure individual and collaborative reflection for continuous growth.

Mentoring Relationship: Self-Assessment Rubric

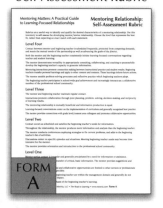

FORM A

Effective Listening Survey

FORM B

Mentoring Skills: Primary Trait Rubric

FORM C

Teaching and Learning Portfolio

FORM D

Teaching and Learning Portfolio: Assessment Rubrics

FORM E

Initial Self-Assessment Profile/ Stem Completions

FORM F

Beginning Teacher Self-Assessment Inventory

FORM G

Learning-focused Growth Plan

FORM H

Learning-focused Growth Plan Tracking Progress

Reflection Journal I

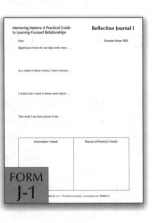

Reflection Journal II

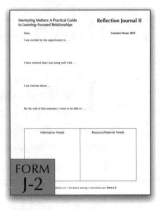

Reflection Journal III

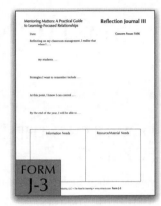

Reflection Journal IV

Reflection Journal V

Reflection Journal VI

Quick Forms

These time-efficient tools scaffold beginning teacher thinking in preparation for meetings and can serve as a third point to focus the conversation. When face-to-face communication is challenging, mentors and their beginning teachers can still check-in using these forms to foster relationship and learning.

3-2-1

3-2-1: Planning

3-2-1: Reflecting

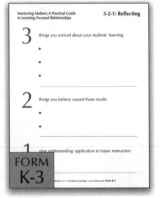

3-2-1: Problem Solving

P+ M- I*

Double Entry Journal

Mindful Memorandum

Video Exercises For Extending Mentoring Skills

These video exercises offer additional practice opportunities for deepening your mentoring skills. Use these forms in concert with the video clips you'll find on our website **www.miravia.com/resources/mm-video-exercises**.

- Paraphrase Exercise Sheet (use with a Video Clip)
- Inquiry Exercises I - Inviting Thinking (use with a Video Clip)
- Inquiry Exercises II - Clarifying Vague Language (use with a Video Clip)
- Learn by Viewing - Processing a Video Model of a Learning-focused Conversation (use Planning or Reflecting Conversation Videos)

Paraphrase Exercise
Sheet

Inquiry: The Invitation

Inquiry: Clarifying Vague
Language

Learn by Viewing

SECTION 8 | References & Resources

Atwater, E. (1992). *Hear you: A listening skills handbook.* New York: Walker and Co.

Ballou, D., & Podgursky, M. (1997). Reforming teacher training and recruitment. *Government Union Review, 17*(4), 1-47.

Bandler, R., & Grinder, J. (1971). *The structure of magic.* Palo Alto, CA: Science and Behavior Books.

Barber, M., & Mourshed, M. (2009). *Shaping the future: How good education systems can become great in the decade ahead.* Report on the International Education Roundtable 11. Singapore: McKinsey & Co., July 7, 2009. www.mckinsey.com/locations/southeastasia/knowledge/ Education_ Roundtable.pdf.

Berliner, D. (2001). Learning about and learning from expert teachers. *International Journal of Educational Research, 35*(5): 463-482.

Boerst, T., Sleep, L., Lowenberg-Ball, D., & Bass, H. (2011). Preparing teachers to lead mathematical discussions. *Teachers College Record 114*(12), 2844-2877.

Bransford, J., Brown, A., & Cocking, R. (Eds.). (1999). *How people learn: Brain, mind, experience, and school.* Washington DC: National Research Council.

Bridges, E. (1990). Evaluation for tenure and dismissal. In J. Millman & L. Darling-Hammond (Eds.), *The new handbook of teacher evaluation: Assessing elementary and secondary teachers.* (pp. 147-157). Newbury Park, CA: Sage.

Calderhead, J. (1996). Teachers: Beliefs and knowledge. In D. Berliner & R. C. Calfee (Eds.), *Handbook of educational psychology.* (pp. 709-725). New York: Simon & Schuster Macmillan.

Carlson, W. S. (1993). Teacher knowledge and discourse control: Quantitative evidence from novice biology teachers' classrooms. *Journal of Research in Science Teaching, 30*(5), 471-481.

Casasanto, D., & Jasmin, L. (2010). Good and bad in the hands of politicians: Spontaneous gestures during positive and negative speech. *PLoS One. July 28; 5*(7): e11805.

Chang, F. Y. (1994). Schoolteachers' moral reasoning. In R. Houston (Ed.), *Handbook of research on teacher education* (pp. 291-310). New York: Macmillan.

Chester, M. D., & Beaudin, B. Q. (1996). Efficacy beliefs of newly hired teachers in urban schools. *American Educational Research Journal, 33*(1), 233-257.

Chi, M., Feltovich, P., & Glaser, R. (1981). Categorization and representation of physics problems by experts and novices. *Cognitive Science 5*: 121-152.

Clark, C. M., & Peterson, P. L. (1986). Teacher thought processes. In M. C. Wittrock (Ed.), *Handbook of research on teaching* (3rd Ed.). (pp. 255-296). New York: Macmillan.

Cogan, M. L. (1973). *Clinical supervision.* Boston: Houghton Mifflin.

Costa, A., & Garmston, R. (2016). *Cognitive Coaching: Developing self-directed leaders and learners* (3rd Ed). Lanham, MD: Rowman & Littlefield.

Covert, J., Williams, L., & Kennedy, W. (1991). Some perceived professional needs of beginning teachers in Newfoundland. *The Alberta Journal of Educational Administration, 27*(1), 3-17.

Coyle, D. (2009). *The talent code: Greatness isn't born. It's grown.* New York: Bantam Books.

Dagenais, J. (1995). *Some tentative mentoring program standards.* The Mentoring Leadership and Resource Network.

Daloz, L. A. (2012). *Mentor: Guiding the journey of adult learners.* San Francisco: Jossey-Bass.

Darling-Hammond, L., & McLaughlin, M. V. (1996). Policies that support professional development in an era of reform. In M. V. McLaughlin & I. Oberman (Eds.), *Teacher learning: New policies and practices.* New York: Teachers College Press.

Darling-Hammond, L. (1996). The quiet revolution: Rethinking teacher development. *Educational Leadership, 53*(6), 4-11.

Darling-Hammond, L. (1997). *The right to learn.* San Francisco: Jossey-Bass.

Darling-Hammond, L. (1998). Teachers and teaching: Testing policy hypotheses from a national commission report. *Educational Researcher, 27*(1), 5-15.

Darling-Hammond, L., & Bransford, J. (2005) *Preparing teachers for a changing world: What teachers should learn and be able to do.* San Francisco: Jossey-Bass.

Duhigg, C. (2012). *The power of habit: Why we do what we do in life and business.* New York: Random House.

Elgin, S. H. (2000). *The gentle art of verbal self-defense.* New York: Prentice Hall.

Ericsson, K. A. (2006). The influence of experience and deliberate practice on the development of superior expert performance. In K. A. Ericsson, N. Charness, P. J. Feltovich, & R. R. Hoffman (Eds.), *The Cambridge handbook of expertise and expert performance* (683-703). New York: Cambridge University Press.

Ericsson, A., & Pool, R. (2016) *Peak: Secrets from the new science of expertise.* New York: Houghton Mifflin Harcourt.

Erikson, E. (1982). *The life cycle completed.* New York: Norton.

Eisner, E. W. (1994). *The educational imagination: On the design and evaluation of school programs.* New York: Macmillan.

Feiman-Nemser, S., Carver, C., Schwille, S., & Yusko, B. (1999). Beyond support: Taking new teachers seriously as learners. In M. Scherer (Ed.), *A Better Beginning* (pp. 3-12). Alexandria VA: Association for Supervision and Curriculum Development.

Fessler, R., & Christensen, J. (1992). *The teacher career cycle: Understanding and guiding the professional development of teachers.* Boston: Allyn & Bacon.

Fisher, D., & Frey, N. (2007). Implementing a school-wide literacy framework: Improving achievement in an urban elementary school. *The Reading Teacher, 61*(1), 32-43.

Fuller, F. (1969). Concerns of teachers: A developmental conceptualization. *American Education Research Journal, 6*(2), 207-226.

Galvez-Hjornevik, C. (1986). Mentoring among teachers: A review of literature. (Report No. SPO26700). Austin, TX: *Journal of Teacher Education.* (ERIC No. ED 262 032).

Ganser, T. (1994). *The impact of time and place in mentoring.* Whitewater, WI: University of Wisconsin.

Gay, G., & Howard, T. (2000). Multicultural teacher education for the 21ˢᵗ century. *Teacher Education, 53*(2), 106-116.

Geary, J. (2011). *I is an other: The secret life of metaphor and how it shapes the way we see the world.* New York: HarperCollins.

Gilligan, C. (1982). *In a different voice.* Cambridge, MA: Harvard University Press.

Glickman, C., Gordon, S., & Ross-Gordon, J. (1995). *Supervision of instruction* (3ʳᵈ ed.). Boston: Allyn & Bacon.

Gold, Y. (1996). Beginning teacher support: Attrition, mentoring and induction. In J. Sikula (Ed.), *Second handbook of research on teacher education* (pp. 548-594). New York: Macmillan.

Goldin-Meadow, S. (2003). *Hearing gesture: How hands help us think.* Cambridge, MA: Harvard University Press.

Goldin-Meadow, S., & Wagner, S. (2005). How our hands help us learn. *Trends in Cognitive Sciences, 9*(5), 234-241.

Goodwin, B. (2012). Research says/New teachers face three common challenges. *Educational Leadership, 69*(8), 84-85.

Graham, L. (2010). The neuroscience of resilience: Attunement. http://loveandlifetoolbox.com/the-neuroscience-of-resilience-attunement/

Grinder, M. (1997). ENVoY: *A personal guide to classroom management.* Battleground WA: Michael Grinder & Associates.

Grinder, M. (2006). *Charisma: The art of relationships.* Battleground Ground, WA: Michael Grinder & Associates.

Hattie, J. (2008). *Visible learning: A synthesis of over 800 meta-analyses relating to achievement.* New York: Routledge.

Hayakawa, S. (1964). *Language in thought and action.* NY: Harcourt, Brace & World.

Hill, H., Rowan, B., & Ball, D. (2005). Effects of teachers' mathematical knowledge for teaching on student achievement. *American Educational Research Journal, 42*(2), 371-406.

Huling-Austin, L., Putman, S., & Galvey-Hjornevik (1986). *Model teacher induction project study findings.* (Report No. 7212). Austin, TX: University of Texas at Austin, R & D Center for Teacher Education.

Hunt, D. (1971). *Matching models of education*. Toronto, Ontario: Institute for Studies in Education.

Hunt, D. E. (1976). Teachers' adaptation: Reading and flexing to students. *Journal of Teacher Education, 27,* 268-275.

Hunt, D. E. (1981). Teachers' adaptation: Reading and flexing to students. In B. Joyce, C. Brown, & L. Peck (Eds.), *Flexibility in teaching (pp. 59-71).* New York: Longman.

Ingersoll, R., & Strong, M. (2011). The impact of induction and mentoring programs for beginning teachers: A critical review of the research. *Review of Educational Research, 81*(2), 201-233.

Ingersoll, R. (June 1998). *The problem of out-of-field teaching.* [online]. http://www.pdkintl.org/kappan/king9806.htm

Jacob, B., & Rockoff, J. (2011). Organizing schools to improve student achievement: Start times, grade configurations, and teacher assignments. (Vol. 2011-08). Washington DC: Brookings Institution. https://www.brookings.edu/research/organizing-schools-to-improve-student-achievement-start-times-grade-configurations-and-teacher-assignments/

Johnson, P., & Umstattd, J. (1932). The classroom difficulties of beginning teachers. *The School Review, 40*(9), 682-686.

Jones, V. (1996). Classroom management. In J. P. Sikula, T. J. Buttery, & E. Guyton (Eds.), *Handbook of research on teacher education* (pp. 503-521). New York: Simon & Schuster Macmillan.

Joyce, B., & Showers, B. (1995). *Student achievement through staff development* (2nd ed.). New York: Longman.

Joyce, B., & Weil, M. (1996). *Models of teaching.* Englewood Cliffs, NJ: Prentice-Hall.

King, S. H., & Bey, T. M. The need for urban teacher mentors. *Education and Urban Society, 28*(1), 3-10.

King, P., & Kitchener, K. (1994). *Developing reflective judgment: Understanding and promoting intellectual growth and critical thinking in adolescents and adults.* San Francisco: Jossey-Bass.

Kutsyuruba, B., Godden, L., Covell, L., Matheson, I., & Walker, K. (2016). Understanding the contextual factors within teacher induction and mentoring programs: An international systematic review of research http://educ.queensu.ca/sites/webpublish.queensu.ca.educwww/files/files/People/Faculty/Systematic%20Review%20Teacher%20Induction%20and%20Mentoring.pdf

Lee, O., Maerten-Rivera, J., Penfield, R., LeRoy, K., & Secada, W. (2008). Science achievement of English language learners in urban elementary schools: Results of a first-year professional development intervention. *Journal of Research in Science Teaching, 45*(1), 31-52.

Leinhardt, G., & Greeno, J. (1986). The cognitive skill of teaching. *Journal of Educational Psychology, 78,* 75-95.

Lipton, L., & Wellman, B. (2000). *Pathways to understanding: Patterns and practices in the learning-focused classroom.* Sherman, CT: MiraVia, LLC.

Lipton, L., & Wellman, B. (2015). *Leading groups: Effective strategies for building professional community.* Charlotte, VT: MiraVia, LLC.

Marzano, R. J. (1992). *A different kind of classroom: Teaching with dimensions of learning.* Alexandria, VA: Association for Supervision and Curriculum Development.

Marzano, R. J., Pickering, D. J., & Pollock, E. (2001). *Classroom instruction that works: Research-based strategies for increasing student achievement.* Alexandria, VA: Association for Supervision and Curriculum Development.

Marzano, R. (2007). *The art and science of teaching: A comprehensive framework for effective instruction.* Alexandria, VA: Association for Supervision and Curriculum Development.

McAllister, G., & Irvine, J. J. (2000). Cross-cultural competency and multicultural teacher education. *Review of Educational Research, 70*(1), 3-24.

McLaughlin, M., Vogt, M., Anderson, J., Dumez, J., Peter, M., & Hunter, A. (1998). *Portfolio models: Reflections across the teaching profession.* Norwood, MA: Christopher-Gordon Publishers, Inc.

McNeill, D. (2005). *Gesture and thought.* Chicago: University of Chicago Press.

Moir, E. (1999). The stages of a teacher's first year. In M. Scherer (Ed.), *Better beginnings: Supporting and mentoring new teachers* (pp. 19-23). Alexandria, VA: Association for Supervision and Curriculum Development.

National Center for Research on Teacher Learning (1999). *Findings on learning to teach.* East Lansing, MI: College of Education, Michigan State University.

National Center for Research on Teacher Learning (1999). *Learning from mentors.* East Lansing, MI: College of Education, Michigan State University.

National Commission on Teaching and America's Future. (1997). *Doing what matters most: Investing in quality teaching.* New York: National Commission on Teaching and America's Future.

Odell, S. (1989). Developing support program for beginning teachers. In R. A. Edelfelt (Ed). *Assisting the beginning teacher* (pp. 3-24). Reston, VA: Association of Teacher Educators.

Odell, S., & Ferraro, D. (1992). Teacher mentoring and teacher retention. *Journal of Teacher Education, 43*(3), 200-204.

Pajares, M. F. (1992). Teachers' beliefs and educational research: Cleaning up a messy construct. *Review of Educational Research, 62*(3), 307-332.

Raths, J., & McAninch, A. C. (2003). *Teacher beliefs and classroom performance: The impact of teacher education.* Greenwich, CT: Information Age Publishing.

Reiman, A. J., Bostick, D., Cooper, J., & Lassiter, J. (1995). Counselor and teacher-led support groups for beginning teachers: A cognitive-developmental perspective. *Elementary School Guidance and Counseling, 30*(2), 105-117.

Reiman, A., & Thies-Sprinthall, L. (1998). *Mentoring and supervision for teacher development.* New York: Addison-Wesley Longman.

Rizzolatti, G., & Arbib, M. (1998). Language within our grasp. *Trends in Neuroscience, 21*(5), 188-194.

Rowe, M. B. (1986 January-February). Wait time: Slowing down may be a way of speeding up! *Journal of Teacher Education,* 43-49.

Sadler, P., Sonnert, G., Coyle, H., Cook-Smith, N., & Miller, J. (2013). The influence of teachers' knowledge on student learning in middle school physical science classrooms. *American Education Research Journal, 50*(8), 1020-1049.

Saphier, J., Haley-Speca, M., & Gower, B. (2018). *The skillful teacher: Building your teaching skills.* Carlisle, MA: Research for Better Teaching.

Shanker, S. (2017). *Self-regulation: How to help your child (and you) break the stress cycle and successfully engage with life.* New York: Penguin Books.

Schon, D. (1983). *The reflective practitioner: How professionals think in action.* New York: Basic Books.

Schon, D. (1987). *Educating the reflective practitioner.* San Francisco: Jossey-Bass.

Shavelson, R. (1986). *Interactive decision making: Some thoughts on teacher cognition.* Paper presented at the First International Congress on Teacher Thinking and Decision Making, La Rabida, Huelva, Seville, Spain, June.

Shea, G. F. (1997). *Mentoring: How to develop successful mentor behaviors.* Los Altos, CA: Crisp Publications, Inc.

Shulman, L. S. (1987). Knowledge and teaching: Foundations of the new reform. *Harvard Educational Review, 57*(1), 1-22.

Snow, C., Griffin, P., & Burns, M. (Eds.). *Knowledge to support the teaching of reading: Preparing teachers for a changing world.* San Francisco: Jossey-Bass.

Spalding, E., Klecka, C., Lin, E., Wang, J., & Odell, S. (2011). Learning to teach: It's complicated but it's not magic. *Journal of Teacher Education, 62*(1), 3-7.

Sprinthall, N., Reiman, A. & Thies-Sprinthall, L. (1993). Roletaking and reflection: Promoting the conceptual and moral development of teachers. *Learning and Individual Differences, 5*(4), 283-299.

Surowiecki, J. (2014). Better all the time: How the "performance revolution" came to athletics and beyond. *The New Yorker.* November 10, 2014, 81-85.

Swanson, H. L., O'Connor, J. E., & Cooney, J. B. (1990). An information processing analysis of expert and novice teachers' problem-solving. *American Educational Research Journal, 27*(3), 533-556.

Thies-Sprinthall, L., & Gerier, E. (1990). Support groups for novice teachers. *Journal of Staff Development, 11*(4), 18-22.

Tschannen-Moran, M., Hoy, A. W., & Hoy, W. K. (1998). Teacher efficacy: Its meaning and measure. *Review of educational research, 68*(2), 202-248.

Turkle, S. (2015). *Reclaiming conversation: The power of talk in a digital age.* New York: Penguin Books.

U.S. Department of Education. National Center for Education Statistics. (1994b). *Qualifications of the public teacher workforce: 1988 and 1991.* Statistical Analysis Report No. 95-665, by S. A. Bobbitt and M. M. McMillen. Washington, DC: U.S. Government Printing Office.

U.S. Department of Education. National Center for Education Statistics. (1996a). *National assessment of teacher quality.* Working Paper No. 96-24, by R. M. Ingersoll. Washington, DC: U.S. Government Printing Office.

U.S. Department of Education. National Center for Education Statistics. (1996b). *Out-of-field teaching and educational quality.* Statistical Analysis Report No. 96-040, by R. M. Ingersoll. Washington, DC: U.S. Government Printing Office.

U.S. Department of Education. National Center for Education Statistics. (1997). *America's teachers: Profile of a profession, 1993-94.* NCES 97-460, by R. R. Henke, S. P. Choy, X. Chen, S. Geis, M. N. Alt, and S. P. Broughman. Washington, DC: U.S. Government Printing Office.

U.S. Department of Education. National Center for Education Statistics (1998a). *The TIMSS videotape classroom study: Methods and findings from an exploratory research project on eighth-grade mathematics instruction in Germany, Japan, and the United States.* Research and Development Report No. 98-047, by J. W. Stigler, P. Gonzales, T. Kawanaka, S. Knoll, and A. Serrano. Washington, DC: U.S. Government Printing Office.

Vygotsky, L. (1978). *Mind in society: The development of higher psychological processes.* Cambridge, MA: Harvard University Press.

Wellman, B. , & Lipton, L. (2017). *Data-driven dialogue: A facilitator's guide to collaborative inquiry.* Charlotte. VT: MiraVia LLC.

Wenglinsky, H. (2000). *How teaching matters: Bringing the classroom back into discussions of teacher quality.* Princeton, NJ: Educational Testing Service.

Wey, H. (1951). Difficulties of beginning teachers. *The School Review, 59*(1), 32-37.

Wiggins, G., & McTighe, J. (2005). *Understanding by design* (2nd Ed.). Alexandria, VA: Association for Supervision and Curriculum Development.

Wiliam, D. (2016). *Leadership for teacher learning: Creating a culture where all teachers improve so that all students succeed.* West Palm Beach, FL: Learning Sciences International.

Wolff, C., van den Bogert, N., Jarodzka, H., & Boshuizen, H. (2015). Keeping an eye on learning: Differences between expert and novice teachers' representations of classroom management events. *Journal of Teacher Education, 66*(1), 68-85.

Zins, J., Bloodworth, M., Weissberg, R., & Walberg, H. (2004). The scientific base linking social and emotional learning to school success. In J. Zins, R. Weissberg, M. Wang, & H. Walberg (Eds.), *Building academic success on social and emotional learning: What does the research say?* (pp.191-210). New York: Teachers College Press.

Online Resources

The following links are offered for your review and information. They do not necessarily represent the authors' views or endorsement. Please let us know if any of these links are especially valuable, or are no longer accessible.

American Federation of Teachers: www.aft.org
> A variety of print and on-line resources for mentors and their beginning teachers.

Beginning Teacher Resources: http://www.teachingfirst.net/BegTeacher.htm
> Links to a variety of sites with useful tools and tips.

Mentor Bibliography: www.teachermentors.com
> Recommended reading in a variety of categories pertinent to beginning teachers and their mentors.

Mentor Support Center: www.teachers.net
> Chat boards in category-specific chats such as beginning teachers.

National Board for Professional Teaching Standards. What teachers should know and be able to do: www.nbpts.org

National Education Association: www.nea.org
> A variety of resources and current research on teaching and induction including:

> The New Teacher Center, University of California Santa Cruz: www.newteachercenter.org
> Multiple resources for mentors and beginning teachers including a free newsletter and other full-text resources.

> Promising Practices: New Ways to Improve Teacher Quality www.ed. gov/teachers/become/about/survivalguide/conclusion.html which includes a full chapter on The Induction of New Teachers

> Resources for Teacher Leadership from The Education Development Center. Links for Mentoring and Coaching. http://teacherleadership.edc.org/mentoring.asp

TeacherTube: www.teachertube.com
> A YouTube channel loaded with videos on a wide variety of topics of interest to teachers at all levels of experience.

U.S. Department of Education: www.ed.gov/index.jsp
> A wealth of resources targeted for induction programs, including:

> The Survival Guide for New Teachers https://www2.ed.gov/teachers/become/about/survivalguide/message. html
> Ideas for new teachers for effective work with veteran colleagues, parents, principals and teacher educators.

Index

Index *(continued)*

Index *(continued)*

Index *(continued)*

About the Authors

Bruce Wellman, M.Ed, Co-Director of *MiraVia, LLC*

Bruce consults with school systems, professional groups, and organizations throughout the United States, Canada, and internationally presenting workshops and courses for teachers and administrators on the patterns and practices of learning-focused classrooms, learning-focused conversations for supervisors and mentors, data-driven collaborative inquiry, presentation skills, and facilitating and developing groups.

Mr. Wellman is an award-winning writer whose work has been honored by the Education Writers Association and the National Staff Development Council. He is the author and co-author of numerous publications related to organizational and professional development, mentoring, quality teaching, and improving professional cultures. He has served as a classroom teacher, curriculum coordinator, and staff developer in the Oberlin, Ohio and Concord, Massachusetts public schools. He holds a B.A. degree from Antioch College and a M.Ed. from Lesley College. Bruce and his wife Leslie enjoy living up a dirt road in Southern Vermont, where they enjoy natural history, birdwatching, and nature photography.

Contact Bruce at:
229 Coyler Road · Guilford, VT 05301
T: 802.257.4892 · F: 802.257.2403 · E: bwellman@miravia.com

Laura Lipton, Ed.D, Co-Director

Laura is an international consultant whose writing, research, keynotes, and seminars focus on effective and innovative instructional practices and on building professional and organizational capacities for enhanced learning. Laura engages with school districts, public and independent schools, departments of education, and international agencies designing and conducting workshops on organizational and group development, learning-focused instruction, literacy development, and growth oriented supervisory and mentoring practices. She applies her extensive experience with professional learning to workshops and seminars conducted globally on topics including learning-focused relationships, data-driven dialogue, teacher leadership, building professional community, developing high-performing teams, action research, and learning-focused mentoring.

Laura is author and co-author of numerous publications related to organizational and professional development. Laura considers her experience orchestrating an open classroom for first/second graders, directing a K-12 Reading Lab, and providing Related Academics on a large vocational education high school campus to be among the highlights of her professional career. Presently, she lives in Northern Vermont, communing with nature and her yellow lab, Bodhi.

Contact Laura at:
236 Lucy's Lane · Charlotte, VT 05445
T: 802.425.6483 · E: lelipton@miravia.com

Learning Opportunities

The Road to Learning

Professional Development Programs and Services Putting Theory into Practice in Your Schools

MiraVia provides learning-focused professional development programs and services that present practical strategies, useful resources and innovative ideas for thoughtful educators grappling with critical professional issues.

KEYNOTE TOPICS

- Creating Communities of Thought: Enhancing Social Capital
- The Future of Learning

- Professional Community Doesn't Just Happen
- Four Barriers to Data-Driven Decision Making

- Growing Teachers: Five Spheres of Expertise
- The Four Qualities of Learning-focused Supervision

SEMINARS & CONSULTING SERVICES

Developing Learning-Focused Relationships

Target Audience:
Teacher mentors, instructional and content coaches, curriculum specialists and instructional supervisors

Explore the essential concepts, templates and mediational tools for developing effective, learning-focused relationships between growth-oriented educators.

Workshops and seminars include:

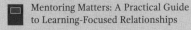 Mentoring Matters: A Practical Guide to Learning-Focused Relationships

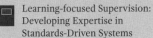 Learning-focused Supervision: Developing Expertise in Standards-Driven Systems

 Based on our book of the same title

Building Professional Community

Target Audience:
School and district leaders, site and district teams, facilitators and group developers

Learn critical skills for developing collaborative school cultures that focus on the learning needs of students and the adults who serve them.

Workshops and seminars include:

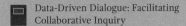 Data-Driven Dialogue: Facilitating Collaborative Inquiry

■ Leading Groups: Effective Strategies for Building Professional Community

■ Learning-Focused Presentations

■ The Facilitator's Toolkit: Balancing Task, Process and Relationship

■ Teacher to Teacher: Working Collaboratively for Student Success

Creating Learning-Focused Classrooms and Schools

Target Audience:
Beginning and experienced classroom teachers, staff developers, instructional leaders

Discover the bridge between current learning theory and effective classroom practice. Our research-based and classroom-tested Pathways Learning Model offers a coherent framework for organizing lessons and units of study.

Workshops and seminars include:

■ Pathways to Understanding: Patterns and Practices in the Learning-Focused Classroom

■ Pathways to Literacy: Reading and Writing in the Content Areas

■ Getting Started, Getting Smarter: Practical Tools for Beginning Teachers

■ Thinking to Learn, Learning to Think

About

 *The Road To Learning*

mira (L.)[MIR-â]: wonderful/amazing via (L.)[VE-â]: way or road

I n 1596, the German astronomer Fabricus saw a third magnitude star in the constellation Cetus, the Whale. As they continued to observe it over the next century, astronomers became aware of its unusual fluctuations, now brighter, now fading, and honored it with the name Mira, the Wonderful.

As a partnership dedicated to continued development for professionals, we connect the constancy of presence and fluctuating brightness with the learning process. We believe that learning means working through the temporary dullness of not knowing, while pursuing the brilliance of new understanding. Our name, and our philosophy, combines this wonder of learning, Mira, with Via, or the road. Our publications, products, and seminars offer pathways to professional insight and growth.